Richard Chenevix Trench

The Study of Words

Lectures Addressed originally to the Pupils at the Diocesan Trainingschool,

Winchester

Richard Chenevix Trench

The Study of Words
Lectures Addressed originally to the Pupils at the Diocesan Trainingschool, Winchester

ISBN/EAN: 9783742800862

Manufactured in Europe, USA, Canada, Australia, Japa

Cover: Foto ©Andreas Hilbeck / pixelio.de

Manufactured and distributed by brebook publishing software (www.brebook.com)

Richard Chenevix Trench

The Study of Words

ON THE

STUDY OF WORDS

LECTURES

ADDRESSED (ORIGINALLY) TO THE PUPILS AT

THE DIOCESAN TRAINING-SCHOOL, WINCHESTER

BY

RICHARD CHENEVIX TRENCH, D.D.

ARCHBISHOP OF DUBLIN

'Language is the armoury of the human mind, and at once contains
the trophies of its past, and the weapons of its future, conquests.'
COLERIDGE

TWELFTH EDITION, CAREFULLY REVISED

London
MACMILLAN AND CO.
1867

The right of translation and reproduction is reserved

PREFACE
TO
THE FIRST EDITION

THESE lectures will not, I trust, be found any where to have left out of sight seriously, or for long, the peculiar needs of those for whom they were originally intended, and to whom they were primarily addressed. I am conscious indeed, here and there, of a certain departure from my first intention, having been in part seduced to this by a circumstance which I had not in the least contemplated when I obtained permission to deliver them, by finding, namely, that I should have other hearers besides the pupils of the Training School. Some matter adapted for those rather than for these I was thus led to introduce—which afterwards I was unwilling, in preparing for the press, to remove; on the contrary adding to it rather, in the hope of obtaining thus a somewhat wider circle of readers than I could have hoped, had I more rigidly restricted myself in the choice of my materials. Yet I should greatly regret to have admitted so much of this as should deprive these lectures of their fitness for those whose profit in writing and in publishing I had mainly in view, namely, schoolmasters and those preparing to be such.

Had I known any book entering with any fulness, and in a popular manner, into the subject-matter of these pages, and making it its exclusive theme, I might still have delivered these lectures, but should scarcely have sought for them a wider audience than their first, gladly leaving the matter in their hands, whose studies in language had been fuller and riper than my own. But abundant and ready to hand as are the materials for such a book, I did not; while yet it seems to me that the subject is one to which it is beyond measure desirable that their attention, who are teaching, or shall have hereafter to teach, others should be directed; so that they shall learn to regard language as one of the chiefest organs of their own education and that of others. For I am persuaded that I have used no exaggeration in saying, that for many a young man ' his first discovery that words are living powers, has been like the dropping of scales from his eyes, like the acquiring of another sense, or the introduction into a new world,'—while yet all this may be indefinitely deferred, may, indeed, never find place at all, unless there is some one at hand to help for him, and to hasten the process; and he who so does, will ever after be esteemed by him as one of his very foremost benefactors. Whatever may be Horne Tooke's shortcomings (and they are great), whether in details of etymology, or in the philosophy of grammar, or in matters more serious still, yet, with all this, what an epoch in many a student's intellectual life has been his first acquaintance with *The Diversions of Purley*. And they were not among the least of the obligations which the young men of our time owed to Coleridge, that he so often himself weighed words in the balances, and so earnestly pressed upon all with whom his voice went for anything, the profit which they would find in so doing. Nor, with the certainty that I am anticipating much in my little volume, can I refrain from quoting some words which were not present with me during its composition, although I must have been familiar with them long ago; words which express excellently well why it is that these studies profit so much, and which will also explain the motives which induced me to add my little contribution to their furtherance:

'A language will often be wiser, not merely

than the vulgar, but even than the wisest of those who speak it. Being like amber in its efficacy to circulate the electric spirit of truth, it is also like amber in embalming and preserving the relics of ancient wisdom, although one is not seldom puzzled to decipher its contents. Sometimes it locks up truths, which were once well known, but which, in the course of ages, have passed out of sight and been forgotten. In other cases it holds the germs of truths, of which, though they were never plainly discerned, the genius of its framers caught a glimpse in a happy moment of divination. A meditative man cannot refrain from wonder, when he digs down to the deep thought lying at the root of many a metaphorical term, employed for the designation of spiritual things, even of those with regard to which professing philosophers have blundered grossly; and often it would seem as though rays of truth, which were still below the intellectual horizon, had dawned upon the imagination as it was looking up to heaven. Hence they who feel an inward call to teach and enlighten their countrymen, should deem it an important part of their duty to draw out the stores of thought which are already latent in their native language, to purify it from the corruptions which Time brings upon all things, and from which language has no exemption, and to endeavour to give distinctness and precision to whatever in it is confused, or obscure, or dimly seen.'—*Guesses at Truth, First Series*, p. 295.

ITCHENSTOKE : *Oct.* 9, 1851.

CONTENTS.

LECTURE I.
Introductory Lecture 1

LECTURE II.
On the poetry in words 34

LECTURE III.
On the morality in words 54

LECTURE IV.
On the history in words 94

LECTURE V.
On the rise of new words 136

LECTURE VI.
On the distinction of words 185

LECTURE VII.
The schoolmaster's use of words . . . 222

ON

THE STUDY OF WORDS.

INTRODUCTORY LECTURE.

THERE are few who would not readily acknowledge that mainly in worthy books are preserved and hoarded the treasures of wisdom and knowledge which the world has accumulated; and that chiefly by aid of these they are handed down from one generation to another. I shall urge on you in these lectures something different from this; namely, that not in books only, which all acknowledge, nor yet in connected oral discourse, but often also in words contemplated singly, there are boundless stores of moral and historic truth, and no less of passion and imagination, laid up—that from these, lessons of infinite worth may be derived, if only our attention is roused to their existence. I shall urge on you (though with teaching such as you enjoy, the subject will not be new), how well it will repay you to study the words which you are in the habit of using or of meeting, be they such as relate to highest spiritual things, or our common words of the shop and the market, and of all the familiar intercourse of life. It will indeed repay you far better than you can easily believe. I am sure, at least, that for many a young man his first discovery of the fact that words are living powers, are the vesture, yea, even the body, which thoughts weave for themselves, has been like the dropping of scales from his eyes, like the acquiring of another sense, or the introduction into a new world; he is never able to cease wondering at the moral marvels that surround him on every side, and ever reveal themselves more and more to his gaze.

We indeed hear it not seldom said that ignorance is the mother of admiration. No falser word was ever spoken, and hardly a more mischievous one; implying, as it does, that this healthiest exercise of the mind rests, for the most part, on a deceit and a delusion, and that with better knowledge it would cease; while, in truth, for once that ignorance leads us to admire that which with fuller insight we should perceive to be a common thing, and one therefore demanding no such tribute from us, a hundred, nay, a thousand times, it prevents us from admiring that which is admirable indeed. And this is so, whether we are moving in the region of nature, which is the region of God's wonders, or in the region of art, which is the region of man's wonders; and nowhere truer than in this sphere and region of language, which is about to claim us now. Oftentimes here we walk up and down in the midst of intellectual and moral marvels with a vacant eye and a careless mind, even as some traveller passes unmoved over fields of fame, or through cities of ancient renown—unmoved, because utterly unconscious of the lofty deeds which there have been wrought, of the great hearts which spent themselves there. We, like him, wanting the knowledge and insight which would have served to kindle admiration in us, are oftentimes deprived of this pure and elevating excitement of the mind, and miss no less that manifold teaching and instruction which ever lie about our path, and nowhere more largely than in our daily words, if only we knew how to put forth our hands and make it our own. 'What riches,' one exclaims, 'lie hidden in the vulgar tongue of our poorest and most ignorant. What flowers of paradise lie under our feet, with their beauties and their parts undistinguished and undiscerned, from having been daily trodden on.'

And this subject upon which we are thus entering ought not to be a dull or uninteresting one in the handling, or one to which only by an effort you will yield the attention which I shall claim. If it shall prove so, this I fear must be through the fault of my manner of treating it; for certainly in itself there is no study which *may* be made at once more instructive and entertaining than the study of the use, origin, and distinction of words, which is exactly that which I now propose to myself and to you. I remember a very learned scholar, to whom we owe one of our best Greek lexicons, a book which must have cost him years, speaking in the preface to his great work with a just disdain of some, who complained of the irksome drudgery of such toils as those which had engaged him so long,—toils irksome, forsooth, because they only had to do with words; with a just disdain of them who claimed pity for themselves, as though they were so many galley-slaves chained to the oar, or martyrs who had offered themselves to the good of the literary world. He declares that the task of classing, sorting, grouping, comparing, tracing the derivation and usage of words, had been to him no drudgery, but a delight and labour of love.

And if this may be true in regard of a foreign tongue, how much truer ought it to be in regard of our own, of our 'mother tongue,' as we affectionately call it. A great writer not very long departed from us has borne witness at once to the pleasantness and profit of this study. 'In a language,' he says, 'like ours, where so many words are derived from other languages, there are few modes of instruction more useful or more amusing than that of accustoming young people to seek for the etymology or primary meaning of the words they use. There are cases in which more knowledge of more value may be conveyed by the history of a word than by the history of a campaign.'

And, implying the same truth, a popular American author has somewhere characterised language as 'fossil poetry.' He evidently means that just as in some fossil, curious and beautiful shapes of vegetable or animal life, the graceful fern or the finely vertebrated lizard, such as now, it may be, have been extinct for thousands of years, are permanently bound up with the stone, and rescued from that perishing which would have otherwise been theirs,—so in words are beautiful thoughts and images, the imagination and the feeling of past ages, of men long since in their graves, of men whose very names have perished, these, which would so easily have perished too, preserved and made safe for ever. The phrase is a striking one; the only fault which one might be tempted to find with it is, that it is too narrow. Language may be, and indeed is, this 'fossil poetry;' but it may be affirmed of it with exactly the same truth that it is fossil ethics, or fossil history. Words quite as often and as effectually embody facts of history, or convictions of the moral common sense, as of the imagination or passion of men; even as, so far as that moral sense may be perverted, they will bear witness and keep a record of that perversion. On all these points I shall enter at full in after lectures; but I may give by anticipation a specimen or two of what I mean, to make from the first my purpose and plan more fully intelligible to all.

Language then is fossil poetry; in other words, we are not to look for the poetry which a people may possess only in its poems, or its poetical customs, traditions, and beliefs. Many a single word also is itself a concentrated poem, having stores of poetical thought and imagery laid up in it. Examine it, and it will be found to rest on some deep analogy of things natural and things spiritual;

bringing those to illustrate and to give an abiding form and body to these. The image may have grown trite and ordinary now; perhaps through the help of this very word may have become so entirely the heritage of all, as to seem little better than a commonplace; yet not the less he who first discerned the relation, and devised the new word which should express it, or gave to an old, never before but literally used, this new and figurative sense, this man was in his degree a poet —a maker, that is, of things which were not before, which would not have existed but for him, or for some other gifted with equal powers. He who spake first of a 'dilapidated' fortune, what an image must have risen up before his mind's eye of some falling house or palace, stone detaching itself from stone, till all had gradually sunk into desolation and ruin. Or he who to that Greek word which signifies 'that which will endure to be held up to and judged by the sunlight,' gave first its ethical signification of 'sincere,' 'truthful,' or as we sometimes say 'transparent,' can we deny to him the poet's feeling and eye? Many a man had gazed, we are sure, at the jagged and indented mountain ridges of Spain, before one called them 'sierras' or 'saws,' the name by which now they are known, as *Sierra* Morena, *Sierra* Nevada; but that man coined his imagination into a word which will endure as long as the everlasting hills which he named.

But it was said just now that words often contain a witness for great moral truths—God having

pressed such a seal of truth upon language, that
men are continually uttering deeper things than
they know, asserting mighty principles, it may be
asserting them against themselves, in words that
to them may seem nothing more than the current
coin of society. Thus to what grand moral purposes Bishop Butler turns the word 'pastime;'
how solemn the testimony which he compels the
world, out of its own use of this word, to render
against itself—obliging it to own that its amuse-
ments and pleasures do not really satisfy the mind
and fill it with the sense of an abiding and satis-
fying joy; * they are only 'pastime;' they serve
only, as this word confesses, to *pass* away the *time*,
to prevent it from hanging, an intolerable burden,
on men's hands: all which they can do at the
best is to prevent men from discovering and
attending to their own internal poverty and dis-
satisfaction and want. He might have added
that there is the same acknowledgment in the

---

* *Sermon* xiv. *Upon the Love of God.* Curiously enough, Montaigne has, in his *Essays*, drawn the same testimony out of the word: 'This ordinary phrase of Pass-time, and passing away the time, represents the custom of those wise sort of people, who think they cannot have a better account of their lives, than to let them run out and slide away, to pass them over and to baulk them, and as much as they can, to take no notice of them and to shun them, as a thing of troublesome and con-temptible quality. But I know it to be another kind of thing, and find it both valuable and commodious even in its latest decay, wherein I now enjoy it, and nature has delivered it into our hands in such and so favourable circumstances that we commonly com-plain of ourselves, if it be troublesome to us or slide unprofitable away.'

word 'diversion,' which means no more than that which *diverts* or turns us aside from ourselves, and in this way helps us to forget ourselves for a little. And thus it would appear that, even according to the world's own confession, all which it proposes is—not to make us happy, but a little to prevent us from remembering that we are unhappy, to *pass* away our *time*, to divert us from ourselves. While on the other hand we declare that the good which will really fill our souls and satisfy them to the uttermost, is not in us, but without us and above us, in the words which we use to set forth any transcending delight. Take three or four of these words—'transport,' 'rapture,' 'ravishment,' 'ecstasy,'—'transport,' that which *carries* us, as 'rapture,' or 'ravishment,' that which *snatches* us out of and above ourselves; and 'ecstasy' is very nearly the same, only drawn from the Greek.

And not less, where a perversion of the moral sense has found place, words preserve oftentimes a record of this perversion. We have a signal example of this, in the use, or rather misuse, of the word 'religion,' during all the ages of Papal domination in Europe. A 'religious' person did not mean any one who felt and allowed the bonds that bound him to God and to his fellow-men, but one who had taken peculiar vows upon him, a member of one of the monkish orders; a 'religious' house did not mean, nor does it now mean in the Church of Rome, a Christian household, ordered in the fear of God, but a house in which these persons were gathered together according to the rule of some man. A 'religion' meant not a service of God, but a monastic order; and taking the monastic vows was termed going into a 'religion.' What a light does this one word so used throw on the entire state of mind and habits of thought in those ages! That then was 'religion,' and nothing else was deserving of the name! And 'religious' was a title which might not be given to parents and children, husbands and wives, men and women fulfilling faithfully and holily in the world the several duties of their stations, but only to those who had devised such a self-chosen service for themselves.* So too that 'lewd,' meaning at one time no more than 'lay,' or unlearned,—the 'lewd' people being the lay people,—should come to signify the sinful, the vicious, is very worthy of note. How forcibly we are reminded here of that saying of the Pharisees: 'This people which knoweth not the law is cursed;' how much of their spirit must have been at work before the word could have acquired this secondary meaning.

But language is fossil history as well. What a record of great social revolutions, revolutions in

---

* A reviewer in *Fraser's Magazine*, Dec. 1851, doubts whether I have not here pushed my assertion too far. So far from this, it was not merely 'the popular language' which this corruption had invaded, but a decree of the great Fourth Lateran Council (A.D. 1215), forbidding the further multiplication of monastic Orders, runs thus: Ne nimia *religionum* diversitas gravem in Ecclesiâ Dei confusionem inducat, firmiter prohibemus, ne quis de cetero novam *religionem* inveniat, sed quicunque voluerit ad *religionem* converti, unam de approbatis assumat.

nations and in the feelings of nations, the one word 'frank' contains, which is used, as we all know, to express aught that is generous, straightforward, and free. The Franks, I need not remind you, were a powerful German tribe, or association of tribes, who gave themselves this proud name of the 'franks' or the free; and who, at the breaking up of the Roman Empire, possessed themselves of Gaul, to which they gave their own name. They were the ruling conquering people, honourably distinguished from the Gauls and degenerate Romans among whom they established themselves by their independence, their love of freedom, their scorn of a lie; they had, in short, the virtues which belong to a conquering and dominant race in the midst of an inferior and conquered one. And thus it came to pass that by degrees the name 'frank' indicated not merely a national, but involved a moral, distinction as well; and a 'frank' man was synonymous not merely with a man of the conquering German race, but was an epithet applied to any man possessed of certain high moral qualities, which for the most part appertained to, and were found only in, men of that stock; and thus in men's daily discourse, when they speak of a person as being 'frank,' or when they use the words 'franchise,' 'enfranchisement,' to express civil liberties and immunities, their language here is the outgrowth, the record, and the result of great historic changes, bears testimony to facts of history, whereof it may well happen that the speakers have never heard.* The word 'slave' has undergone a process entirely analogous, although in an opposite direction. 'The martial superiority of the Teutonic races enabled them to keep their slave markets supplied with captives taken from the Sclavonic tribes. Hence, in all the languages of Western Europe, the once glorious name of Sclave has come to express the most degraded condition of man. What centuries of violence and warfare does the history of this word disclose.'†

Having given by anticipation this handful of examples in illustration of what in these lectures I propose, I will, before proceeding further, make a few observations on a subject, which, if we would go at all to the root of the matter, we can scarcely leave altogether untouched,—I mean the origin of language; in which however we will not entangle ourselves deeper than we need. There are, or rather there have been, two theories about this. One, and that which rather has been than now is, for few maintain it still, would put language on the same level with the various arts and inventions with which man has gradually adorned and enriched his life. It would make him by degrees to have invented it, just as he might have invented any of these, for himself;

---

* 'Frank,' though thus originally a German word, only came back to Germany from France in the seventeenth century. With us it is found in the sixteenth; but scarcely earlier.

† J. Taylor, *Words and Places*, p. 441: cf. Gibbon, *Decline and Fall*, c. 55.

and from rude imperfect beginnings, the inarticulate cries by which he expressed his natural wants, the sounds by which he sought to imitate the impression of natural objects upon him, little by little to have arrived at that wondrous organ of thought and feeling, which his language is often to him now.

It might, I think, be sufficient to object to this explanation, that language would then be an *accident* of human nature; and, this being the case, that we certainly should somewhere encounter tribes sunken so low as not to possess it; even as there is no human art or invention, though it be as simple and obvious as the preparing of food by fire, but there are those who have fallen below its exercise. But with language it is not so. There have never yet been found human beings, not the most degraded horde of South-African bushmen, or Papuan cannibals, who did not employ this means of intercourse with one another. But the more decisive objection to this view of the matter is, that it hangs together with, and is indeed an essential part of, that theory of society, which is contradicted alike by every page of Genesis, and every notice of our actual experience—the 'urang-utang theory,' as it has been so happily termed—that, I mean, according to which the primitive condition of man was the savage one, and the savage himself the seed out of which in due time the civilized man was unfolded; whereas, in fact, so far from being this living seed, he might more justly be considered as a dead withered leaf, torn violently away from the great trunk of humanity, and with no more power to produce anything nobler than himself out of himself, than that dead withered leaf to unfold itself into the oak of the forest. So far from being the child with the latent capabilities of manhood, he is himself rather the man prematurely aged, and decrepit, and outworn.

But the truer answer to the inquiry how language arose, is this: God gave man language, just as He gave him reason, and just because He gave him reason; for what is man's *word* but his *reason*, coming forth that it may behold itself? They are indeed so essentially one and the same that the Greek language has one word for them both. He gave it to him, because he could not be man, that is, a social being, without it. Yet this must not be taken to affirm that man started at the first furnished with a full-formed vocabulary of words, and as it were with his first dictionary and first grammar ready-made to his hands. He did not thus begin the world *with names* but *with the power of naming*: for man is not a mere speaking machine; God did not teach him words, as one of us teaches a parrot, from without; but gave him a capacity, and then evoked the capacity which He gave. Here, as in everything else that concerns the primitive constitution, the great original institutes, of humanity, our best and truest lights are to be gotten from the study of the three first chapters of Genesis; and you will observe that there it is not God who imposed the first names on the creatures, but Adam—Adam, however, at the direct suggestion of his Creator. *He* brought them all, we are told, to Adam, 'to see what he would call them; and whatsoever Adam called every living creature, that was the name thereof' (Gen. ii. 19). Here we have the clearest intimation of the origin, at once divine and human, of speech; while yet neither is so brought forward as to exclude or obscure the other.

And so far we may concede a limited amount of right to those who have held a progressive acquisition, on man's part, of the power of embodying thought in words. I believe that we should conceive the actual case most truly, if we conceived this power of naming things and expressing their relations, as one laid up in the depths of man's being, one of the divine capacities with which he was created: but one (and in this differing from those which have produced in various people various arts of life), which could not remain dormant in him, for man could be only man through its exercise; which therefore did rapidly bud and blossom out from within him at every solicitation from the world without, or from his fellow-man; as each object to be named appeared before his eyes, each relation of things to one another arose before his mind. It was not merely the possible, but the necessary, emanation of the spirit with which he had been endowed. Man makes his own language, but he makes it as the bee makes its cells, as the bird its nest; he cannot do otherwise.

How this latent power evolved itself first, how this spontaneous generation of language came to pass, is a mystery, even as every act of creation is of necessity such; and as a mystery all the deepest inquirers into the subject are content to leave it. Yet we may perhaps a little help ourselves to the realizing of what the process was, and what it was not, if we liken it to the growth of a tree springing out of, and unfolding itself from, a root, and according to a necessary law—that root being the divine capacity of language with which man was created, that law being the law of highest reason with which he was endowed: if we liken it to this rather than to the rearing of a house, which a man should slowly and painfully fashion for himself with dead timbers combined after his own fancy and caprice; and which little by little improved in shape, material, and size, being first but a log house, answering his barest needs, and only after centuries of toil and pain growing for his sons' sons into a stately palace for pleasure and delight.

Were it otherwise, were the savage the primitive man, we should then find savage tribes furnished, scantily enough, it might be, with the elements of speech, yet at the same time with its fruitful beginnings, its vigorous and healthful germs. But what does their language on close inspection prove? In every case what they are themselves, the remnant and ruin of a better and a nobler past. Fearful indeed is the impress of degradation which is stamped on the language of the savage, more fearful perhaps even than that which is stamped upon his form. When wholly letting go the truth, when long and greatly sinning against light and conscience, a people has thus gone the downward way, has been scattered off by some violent catastrophe from those regions of the world which are the seats of advance and progress, and driven to its remote isles and further corners, then as one nobler thought, one spiritual idea after another has perished from it, the words also that expressed these have perished too. As one habit of civilization has been let go after another, the words which those habits demanded have dropped as well, first out of use, and then out of memory, and thus after a while have been wholly lost.

Moffat, in his *Missionary Labours and Scenes in South Africa*, gives us a very remarkable example of the disappearing of one of the most significant words from the language of a tribe sinking ever deeper in savagery; and with the disappearing of the word, of course, the disappearing as well of the great spiritual fact and truth whereof that word was at once the vehicle and the guardian. The Bechuanas, a Caffre tribe, employed formerly the word 'Morimo,' to designate 'Him that is above,' or 'Him that is in Heaven,' and attached to the word the notion of a supreme Divine Being. This word, with the spiritual idea corresponding to it, Moffat found to have vanished from the language of the present generation, although here and there he could meet with an old man, scarcely one or two in a thousand, who remembered in his youth to have heard speak of 'Morimo;' and this word, once so deeply significant, only survived now in the spells and charms of the so-called rain-makers and sorcerers, who misused it to designate a fabulous ghost, of whom they told the absurdest and most contradictory things.

And as there is no such witness to the degradation of the savage as the brutal poverty of his language, so is there nothing that so effectually tends to keep him in the depths to which he has fallen. You cannot impart to any man more than the words which he understands either now contain, or can be made, intelligibly to him, to contain. Language is as truly on one side the limit and restraint of thought, as on the other side that which feeds and unfolds thought. Thus it is the ever-repeated complaint of the missionary that the very terms are well-nigh or wholly wanting in the dialect of the savage whereby to impart to him heavenly truths, or indeed even the nobler emotions of the human heart. Dobrizhoffer, the Jesuit missionary, in his curious *History of the Abipones*, tells us that neither these nor the Guarinies, two of the principal native tribes of Brazil, possessed any word in the least corresponding to our 'thanks.' But what wonder, if the feeling of gratitude was entirely absent from their hearts, that they should not have possessed the corresponding word in their vocabularies? Nay, how should they have had it there? And that in this absence lies the true explanation is plain from a fact which the same writer records, that, although inveterate askers, they never showed the slightest sense of obligation or of gratitude, when they obtained what they sought; never saying more than, 'This will be useful to me,' or, 'This is what I wanted.' Dr. Krapf, after laborious researches in some widely extended dialects of East Africa, has remarked in them the same absence of any words expressing the idea of gratitude.

Nor is it only in what they have forfeited and lost, but also in what they have retained or invented, that these languages proclaim their degradation and debasement, and how deeply they and those that speak them have fallen. Thus I have read of a tribe in New Holland, which has no word to signify God, but has one to designate a process by which an unborn child may be destroyed in the bosom of its mother. And I have been informed, on the authority of one excellently capable of knowing, an English scholar long resident in Van Diemen's Land, that in the native language of that island there are four words to express the taking of human life—one to express a father's killing of a son, another a son's killing of a father, with other varieties of murder; and that in no one of these lies the slightest moral reprobation, or sense of the deep-lying distinction between to 'kill' and to 'murder;'

while at the same time, of that language so richly and so fearfully provided with expressions for this extreme utterance of hate, he also reports that a word for 'love' is wanting in it altogether. Yet with all this, ever and anon in the midst of this wreck and ruin, there is that in the language of the savage, some subtle distinction, some curious allusion to a perished civilization, now utterly unintelligible to the speaker; or some other note, which proclaims his language to be the remains of a dissipated inheritance, the rags and remnants of a robe which was a royal one once. The fragments of a broken sceptre are in his hand, a sceptre wherewith once he held dominion (he, that is, in his progenitors) over large kingdoms of thought, which now have escaped wholly from his sway.*

But while it is thus with him, while this is the downward course of all those that have chosen the downward path, while with every impoverishing and debasing of personal and national life there goes hand in hand a corresponding impoverishment and debasement of language, so on the contrary, where there is advance and progress, where a divine idea is in any measure realizing

---

* See on this matter Tylor, *Early History of Mankind*, pp. 150-190. Among some of the Papuas the faintest rudiments of the family survive; of the tribe no trace whatever; while yet of these one has lately written:—'Sie haben religiöse Gebräuche und Uebungen, welche, mit einigen anderen Erscheinungen in ihrem Leben, mit ihrem jetzigen Culturzustande ganz unvereinbar erscheinen, wenn man darin nicht die Spuren einer früher höhern Bildung erkennen will.'

itself in a people, where they are learning more accurately to define and distinguish, more truly to know, where they are ruling, as men ought to rule, over nature, and compelling her to give up her secrets to them, where new thoughts are rising up over the horizon of a nation's mind, new feelings are stirring at a nation's heart, new facts coming within the sphere of its knowledge, there will language be growing and advancing too. It cannot lag behind; for man feels that nothing is properly his own, that he has not secured any new thought, or entered upon any new spiritual inheritance, till he has fixed it in language, till he can contemplate it, not as himself, but as his word; he is conscious that he must express truth, if he is to preserve it, and still more if he would propagate it among others. 'Names,' as it has been excellently said, 'are impressions of sense, and as such take the strongest hold upon the mind, and of all other impressions can be most easily recalled and retained in view. They therefore serve to give a point of attachment to all the more volatile objects of thought and feeling. Impressions that when past might be dissipated for ever, are by their connexion with language always within reach. Thoughts, of themselves, are perpetually slipping out of the field of immediate mental vision; but the name abides with us, and the utterance of it restores them in a moment.'

Men sometimes complain of the number of new theological terms which the great controversies in which the Church from time to time has

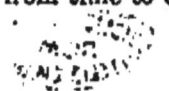

been engaged, have left behind them; but this could not be otherwise, unless the gains through those controversies made, were presently to be lost again. One has lately written well upon this matter: 'The success and enduring influence of any systematic construction of truth, be it secular or sacred, depends as much upon an exact terminology, as upon close and deep thinking itself. Indeed, unless the results to which the human mind arrives are plainly stated, and firmly fixed in an exact phraseology, its thinking is to very little purpose in the end. "Terms," says Whewell, "record discoveries." That which was seen, it may be with crystal clearness, and in bold outline, in the consciousness of an individual thinker, may fail to become the property and possession of mankind at large, because it is not transferred from the individual to the general mind, by means of a precise phraseology and a rigorous terminology. Nothing is in its own nature more fugacious and shifting than thought; and particularly thoughts upon the mysteries of Christianity. A conception that is plain and accurate in the understanding of the first man becomes obscure and false in that of the second, because it was not grasped and firmly held in the form and proportions with which it first came up, and then handed over to other minds, a fixed and scientific quantity.'* And on the necessity of names for the propagation of truth it has been justly observed:

---

* Shedd *History of Christian Doctrine*, vol. i. p. 362.

'Hardly any original thoughts on mental or social subjects ever make their way among mankind, or assume their proper proportions in the minds even of their inventors, until aptly selected words or phrases have as it were nailed them down and held them fast.' This, of course, is as true of an error as of a truth. When the medieval Church invented and allowed the word 'transubstantiation' (and we know exactly the date when it did so), it committed itself to a doctrine from which henceforward it was impossible to recede. The floating error had become a fixed one, and exercised a far mightier influence on the minds of all who received it, than ever else it would have done.

Nor does what has here been said of the manner in which language enriches itself contradict a prior assertion, that man starts with language as God's perfect gift, which he only impairs and forfeits by sloth and sin, according to the same law which holds good in respect of each other of the gifts of heaven. For it was not meant, as indeed was then observed, that men would possess words to set forth feelings which were not yet stirring in them, combinations which they had not yet made, objects which they had not yet seen, relations of which they were not yet conscious; but that up to his needs, (those needs including not merely his animal wants, but all his higher spiritual cravings,) he would find utterance freely. The great logical, or grammatical, framework of language, (for grammar is the logic of speech, even as logic is the grammar of reason,) he would

I. LANGUAGE THE EMBODIMENT OF THOUGHTS. 23

possess, he knew not how; and certainly not as the final result of gradual acquisitions, and of reflexion setting these in order, and drawing general rules from them; but as that rather which alone had made those acquisitions possible; as that according to which he unconsciously worked, filled in this framework by degrees with these later acquisitions of thought, feeling, and experience, as one by one they arrayed themselves in the garment and vesture of words.

Here then is the explanation of the fact that language should be thus instructive for us, that it should yield us so much, when we come to analyse and probe it; and yield us the more, the more deeply and accurately we do so. It is full of instruction, because it is the embodiment, the incarnation, if I may so speak, of the feelings and thoughts and experiences of a nation, yea, often of many nations, and of all which through long centuries they have attained to and won. It stands like the pillars of Hercules, to mark how far the moral and intellectual conquests of mankind have advanced, only not like those pillars, fixed and immovable, but ever itself advancing with the progress of these. The mighty moral instincts which have been working in the popular mind have found therein their unconscious voice; and the single kinglier spirits that have looked deeper into the heart of things have oftentimes gathered up all they have seen into some one word, which they have launched upon the world, and with which they have enriched it for ever—making in that new word a new region of thought to be henceforward in some sort the common heritage of all. Language is the amber in which a thousand precious and subtle thoughts have been safely embedded and preserved. It has arrested ten thousand lightning flashes of genius, which, unless thus fixed and arrested, might have been as bright, but would have also been as quickly passing and perishing, as the lightning. 'Words convey the mental treasures of one period to the generations that follow; and laden with this, their precious freight, they sail safely across gulfs of time in which empires have suffered shipwreck, and the languages of common life have sunk into oblivion.' And for all these reasons far more and mightier in every way is a language than any one of the works which may have been composed in it. For that work, great as it may be, is but the embodying of the mind of a single man, this of a nation. The *Iliad* is great, yet not so great in strength or power or beauty as the Greek language. *Paradise Lost* is a noble possession for a people to have inherited, but the English tongue is a nobler heritage yet.

And short as we may, and indeed must, stop of apprehending all this, there is an obscure sense, or instinct I might call it, in every one of us, of at least some part of this truth. We all of us, whether we have given a distinct account of the matter to ourselves or no, believe that the words which we use, some at least of them, stand in a more or less real relation to the things which they designate,—that they are not arbitrary signs, affixed at random, for which any other might have been substituted as well. And this sense of the significance of names, that they are, or ought to be,—that in a world of absolute truth they ever would be,—the utterance of the innermost character and qualities of the things or persons that bear them, speaking out in various other ways, speaks out in none more clearly than in this—namely, in the amusement and interest which children find in any striking agreement between a name and the person who owns that name—or, which naturally lays hold on their attention far more, in any striking contradiction between the name and the name-bearer; as, for instance, if Mr. Strongitharm is a weakling, or Mr. Black an albino; the first striking from a sense of fitness, the other from one of incongruity.

Nor is this a mere childish entertainment. It continues with us through life; and that its roots lie deep is attested by the earnest use which is often made, and that at the most earnest moments of men's lives, of such agreements or disagreements as these. 'Call me not Naomi,' exclaims the desolate widow—'call me not Naomi [or *pleasantness*]; call me Marah [or *bitterness*], for the Almighty hath dealt very bitterly with me.' She cannot bear the contradiction between the name she bears and the thing she is. Shakespeare, in like manner, reveals his own profound knowledge of the human heart, when he makes old John of Gaunt, worn with long sickness, and now ready to depart, play with his name, and dwell upon the consent between it and his condition; so that when his royal nephew asks him, 'How is it with aged Gaunt?' he answers,

> 'Oh, how that name befits my composition,
> Old *Gaunt* indeed, and *gaunt* in being old—
> *Gaunt* am I for the grave, *gaunt* as the grave—'

with much more in the same fashion; while it is into the mouth of the slight and frivolous king that Shakespeare puts the exclamation of wonder,

> 'Can sick men play so nicely with their names?'

Thus too, if one is engaged in a controversy or quarrel, and his name import something good, an adversary will lay hold of the name, will seek to bring out a real contradiction between it and its bearer, so that he shall appear as one presenting himself under false colours, affecting a merit which is really strange to him. Examples of this are innumerable. For instance, there was one Vigilantius in the early Church;—his name might be interpreted 'the Watchful.' He was engaged in a controversy with Jerome, in regard of certain vigils; which he thought perilous to Christian morality, but of which Jerome was a very eager maintainer; who instantly gave a turn to his name, and proclaimed that he, the enemy of these watches, the friend of slumber and sloth, should have been not Vigilantius, or 'the Watcher,' but Dormitantius, or 'the Sleeper,' rather. It will be seen then that the Greek tragic poet is true to nature when, in his *Prometheus Bound*, he makes Strength tauntingly to remind Prometheus, or The Prudent, how ill his name and the lot which he has made for himself agree, bound as he is with adamantine chains to his rock, and bound as it might seem for ever.

But this hostile use of names, this attempt to place them and their owners in the most intimate connexion, to make, so to speak, the man answerable for his name, we trace still more frequently where the name does not thus need to be reversed; but may be made as it now is, or with very slightest change, to contain a confession of the ignorance, worthlessness, or futility of the bearer. If it implies, or can be made to imply, anything bad, it is instantly laid hold of as expressing the very truth about him. You know the story of Helen of Greece, whom Marlowe's Faust so magnificently apostrophises:

> 'Is this the face that launched a thousand ships,
> And burned the topless towers of Ilium?'

It is no frigid conceit of the Greek poet, when passionately denouncing the ruin which she wrought, he finds that ruin couched and fore-announced in her name—as in English it might be and has been reproduced—

> '*Hell* in her name, and heaven in her looks.'

Pope Hildebrand, in our *Homilies*, is styled 'Brand of Hell,' as setting the world in a blaze; Sanders, the foul-mouthed libeller of Queen Elizabeth, is with more of justice by old Fuller styled 'Slanders rather.' There were two not inconsiderable persons in our Civil Wars, Vane (not the 'young Vane' of Milton and Wordsworth) and Sterry; and one of them, Sterry, was chaplain to the other. Baxter, having occasion to mention them in his profoundly instructive *Narrative of his Life and Times*, and liking neither, cannot forbear to observe, that 'vanity and sterility were never more suitably joined together;' and speaks in another place of 'the vanity of Vane, and the sterility' (this last charge is a singularly unjust one) 'of Sterry.' *

---

* A few more examples in a note. Antiochus Epiphanes, or 'the Illustrious,' is for the Jews, whom he so madly attempted to hellenize, Antiochus Epimanes, or 'the Insane.' Cicero, denouncing Verres, the infamous prætor of Sicily, is too skilful a master of the passions to allow his name to escape him. He was indeed 'Verres,' for he *swept* the province; he was a sweep-net for it (*everriculum in provinciâ*); and then presently, giving altogether another turn to his name, Others, he says, might be partial to 'jus verrinum' (which might mean either Verrine law, or boar sauce), but not he. Tiberius Claudius Nero, charged by the popular voice with being a drunkard, becomes Biberius Caldius Mero. The controversies of the Church with heretics yield only too abundant a supply, and that upon both sides, of examples in this kind. The noble Athanasius is Satanasius for the Arians; and some of St. Cyprian's adversaries did not shrink from so foul a perversion of his name as to call him Κοπριανός, or 'the Dungy.' But then, on the other hand, how often is Pelagius declared by the Church Fathers to be a 'pelagus,' or ocean, of wickedness. It was in vain that the Manichæans changed their master's name from Manes to Manichæus, that so it might not so nearly resemble the word signifying madness in the Greek (*devitantes nomen insaniæ*, Augustine, *De Hær.* 46); they did not thereby escape. Metrophanes, a Patriarch of Constantinople, being counted to have

Where, on the other hand, it is desired to do a man honour, how gladly, in like manner, is his name seized on, if it bears in it anything of an honourable significance, or is capable of an honourable interpretation—men finding in that name a presage and prophecy, an indication and out-speaking, of that which was actually in its bearer. A multitude of examples, many of them beautiful enough, might be brought together in this kind. How often, for instance, and with what effect, the name of Stephen the protomartyr, that name signifying 'the Crown,' was taken as a prophetic intimation of the martyr-crown, which it should be given to him, the first in that noble army, to wear. Irenæus means in Greek 'the Peaceable;' and early Church writers love to remark how fitly the great bishop of Lyons in the second century bore this name, setting forward as he so eminently did the peace of the Church, resolved as he was, so far as in him lay, to preserve the unity of the Spirit in the bond of peace. The Dominicans were well pleased when their name was resolved into Domini canes—the Lord's watch-dogs; who, as such, allowed no heresy to appear without at once giving the alarm, and seeking to chase it away. Fuller, our own Church historian, who played so often on the names of

---

betrayed the interests of the Greek Church, his spiritual mother, in certain negotiations with the Latin, acquired the title of Metrophonos, or 'the Matricide.' It would be curious to know how often the Sorbonne has been likened to a Serbonian bog.

others, has a play made upon his own in some commendatory verses affixed to one of his books:

> 'Thy style is clear and white; thy very name
> Speaks pureness, and adds lustre to the frame.'

John Careless, whose letters are among the most beautiful in Fox's *Book of Martyrs*, writing to Philpot, exclaims 'Oh good master Philpot, which art a principal pot indeed, filled with much precious liquor,—oh pot most happy! of the High Potter ordained to honour.'

These examples I adduce here less for their own sake, than as witnesses for the wide-spread faith of men in the significance of the words and names which they employ. You will not, then, find it a hard and laborious task to persuade your pupils of this. They are prepared to accept, they will be prompt to believe it. And great indeed will be our gains, their gains and ours,—for teacher and taught will for the most part enrich themselves together,—if, having these treasures of wisdom and knowledge lying round about us, so far more precious than mines of Californian gold, we determine that we will make what portion of them we can our own, that we will ask the words which we use to give an account of themselves, to say whence they are, and whither they tend. Then shall we often rub off the dust and rust from what seemed to us but a common token, which as such we had taken and given a thousand times; but which now we shall perceive to be a precious coin, bearing the 'image and superscription' of the great King: then shall we often stand in surprise and in something of shame, while we behold the great spiritual realities which underlie our common speech, the marvellous truths which we have been witnessing *for* in our words, but, it may be, witnessing *against* in our lives. And as you will not find, for so I venture to promise, that this study of words will be a dull one when you undertake it yourselves, as little need you fear that it will prove dull and unattractive, when you seek to make your own gains herein the gains also of those who may be hereafter committed to your charge. Only try your pupils, and mark the kindling of the eye, the lighting up of the countenance, the revival of the flagging attention, with which the humblest lecture upon words, and on the words especially which they are daily using, which are familiar to them at their play or at their church, will be welcomed by them. There is a sense of reality about children which makes them rejoice to discover that there is also a reality about words, that they are not merely arbitrary signs, but living powers; that, to reverse the words of one of England's 'false prophets,' they may be the fool's counters, but are the wise man's money; not, like the sands of the sea, innumerable disconnected atoms, but growing out of roots, clustering in families, connecting and intertwining themselves with all that men have been doing and thinking and feeling from the beginning of the world till now.

And it is of course our English tongue, out of

which mainly we should seek to draw some of the hid treasures which it contains, from which we should endeavour to remove the veil which custom and familiarity have thrown over it. We cannot employ ourselves better. There is nothing that will more help than will this to form an English heart in ourselves and in others. We could scarcely have a single lesson on the growth of our English tongue, we could scarcely follow up one of its significant words, without having unawares a lesson in English history as well, without not merely falling on some curious fact illustrative of our national life, but learning also how the great heart which is beating at the centre of that life was gradually shaped and moulded. We should thus grow too in our feeling of connexion with the past, of gratitude and reverence to it; we should estimate more truly, and therefore more highly, what it has done for us, all that it has bequeathed us, all that it has made ready to our hands. It was something for the children of Israel when they came into Canaan, to enter upon wells which they digged not, and vineyards which they had not planted, and houses which they had not built; but how much greater a boon, how much more glorious a prerogative, for any one generation to enter upon the inheritance of a language which other generations by their truth and toil have made already a receptacle of choicest treasures, a storehouse of so much unconscious wisdom, a fit organ for expressing the subtlest distinctions, the tenderest sentiments, the largest thoughts, and the loftiest imaginations, which the heart of man should at any time conceive. And that those who have preceded us have gone far to accomplish this for us, I shall rejoice if I am able in any degree to make you feel in the lectures which will follow the present.

LECTURE II.

ON THE POETRY IN WORDS.

I SAID in my last lecture, or rather I quoted another who had said, that language is fossil poetry. It is true that for us very often this poetry which is bound up in words has in great part or altogether disappeared. We fail to recognize it, partly from long familiarity with it, partly, it may be, from never having had our attention called to it. None have pointed it out to us; we may not ourselves have possessed the means of detecting it; and thus it has come to pass that we have been close to this wealth, and yet it has not been ours. Margaret has not been for us 'the Pearl,' nor Esther 'the Star,' nor Susanna 'the Lily,'[*] nor Stephen 'the Crown.' 'In our ordinary language,' as Montaigne has well said, 'there are several excellent phrases and metaphors to be met with, of which the beauty is withered by age, and the colour is sullied by too common handling; but that takes nothing from the relish to an under-

---

[*] See Jacob Grimm, *Über Frauennamen aus Blumen*, in his *Kleinere Schriften*, vol. ii. pp. 366-401.

standing man, neither does it derogate from the glory of those ancient authors, who, 'tis likely, first brought those words into that lustre.' We read in one of Molière's most famous comedies of one who was surprised to discover that he had been talking prose all his life without being aware of it. If we knew all, we might be much more surprised to find that we had been talking poetry, without ever having so much as suspected this. For indeed poetry and passion seek to insinuate, and do insinuate themselves everywhere in language; they preside continually at the giving of names; they enshrine and incarnate themselves in these. I devote my present lecture to a few examples and illustrations, by which I would make the truth of this which I have affirmed appear.

'Iliads without a Homer,' some one has called, with a little exaggeration, the beautiful but anonymous ballad poetry of Spain. One may be permitted, perhaps, to push the exaggeration a little further in the same direction, and to apply the same language not merely to a ballad but to a word. For poetry, which is passion and imagination embodying themselves in words, does not necessarily demand a *combination* of words for this. Of this passion and imagination a single word may be the vehicle. As the sun can image itself alike in a tiny dewdrop or in the mighty ocean, and can do it, though on a different scale, as perfectly in the one as in the other, so the spirit of poetry can dwell in and glorify alike a word and an Iliad. Nothing in language is too small, as nothing is too great, for it to fill with its presence. Everywhere it can find, or, not finding, can make, a shrine for itself, which afterwards it can render translucent and transparent with its own indwelling glory. On every side we are beset with poetry. Popular language is full of it, of words used in an imaginative sense, of things called,—and not merely in transient moments of high passion, and in the transfer which at such moments finds place of the image to the thing imaged, but permanently,—by names having immediate reference not to what they are, but to what they are like.

Thus, for example, at Naples it is the ordinary language to call the lesser storm-waves 'pecore,' or sheep, the larger 'cavalloni,' or big horses. Who that has watched the foaming crests, the white manes, as it were, of the larger billows as they advance in measured order, and rank on rank, into the bay, but will own not merely the fitness, but the grandeur, of this last image? Let me illustrate my meaning more at length by the word 'tribulation.' We all know in a general way that this word, which occurs not seldom in Scripture and in the Liturgy, means affliction, sorrow, anguish; but it is quite worth our while to know *how* it means this, and to question the word a little closer. It is derived from the Latin 'tribulum,' which was the threshing instrument or harrow, whereby the Roman husbandman separated the corn from the husks; and 'tribulatio' in its primary significance was the act of this separation.

But some Latin writer of the Christian Church appropriated the word and image for the setting forth of a higher truth; and sorrow, distress, and adversity being the appointed means for the separating in men of whatever in them was light, trivial, and poor from the solid and the true, their chaff from their wheat,* he therefore called these sorrows and trials 'tribulations,' threshings, that is, of the inner spiritual man, without which there could be no fitting him for the heavenly garner. Now in proof of my assertion that a single word is often a concentrated poem, a little grain of pure gold capable of being beaten out into a broad extent of gold-leaf, I will quote, in reference to this very word 'tribulation,' a graceful compôsition by George Wither, a poet of the seventeenth century. You will at once perceive that it is all wrapped up in this word, being from first to last only the expanding of the image and thought which this word has implicitly given; it is as follows:

> 'Till from the straw the flail the corn doth beat,
> Until the chaff be purged from the wheat,
> Yea, till the mill the grains in pieces tear,
> The richness of the flour will scarce appear.
> So, till men's persons great afflictions touch,
> If worth be found, their worth is not so much,
> Because, like wheat in straw, they have not yet
> That value which in threshing they may get.
> For till the bruising flails of God's corrections
> Have threshèd out of us our vain affections;
> Till those corruptions which do misbecome us
> Are by Thy sacred Spirit winnowed from us;

---

* 'Triticum' itself may be connected with tero, tritus.

Until from us the straw of worldly treasures,
Till all the dusty chaff of empty pleasures,
Yea, till His flail upon us He doth lay,
To thresh the husk of this our flesh away;
And leave the soul uncovered; nay, yet more,
Till God shall make our very spirit poor,
We shall not up to highest wealth aspire;
But then we shall; and that is my desire.'

This deeper religious use of the word 'tribulation' was unknown to classical antiquity, belonging exclusively to the Christian writers: and the fact that the same deepening and elevating of the use of words recurs in a multitude of other, and many of them far more signal, instances, is one well deserving to be followed up. Nothing, I am persuaded, would more mightily convince us of the new power which Christianity proved in the world than to compare the meaning which so many words possessed before its rise, and the deeper meaning which they obtained, so soon as they were assumed as the vehicles of its life, the new thought and feeling enlarging, purifying, and ennobling the very words which they employed. This is a subject which I shall have occasion to touch on more than once in these lectures, but is itself well worthy of, as it would afford ample material for, a volume.

On the suggestion of this word 'tribulation,' I will quote two or three words from Coleridge, bearing on the matter in hand. He has said, 'In order to get the full sense of a word, we should first present to our minds the visual image that forms its primary meaning.' What admirable counsel is here! If we would but accustom ourselves to the doing of this, what vast increases of precision and force would all the language which we speak, and which others speak to us, obtain; how often would that which is now obscure at once become clear; how distinct the limits and boundaries of that which is often now confused and confounded! It is difficult to measure the amount of food for the imagination, as well as gains for the intellect, which the observing of this single rule would afford us. Let me illustrate this by one or two examples. We say of such a man that he is 'desultory.' Do we attach any very distinct meaning to the word? Perhaps not. But get at the image on which 'desultory' rests; take the word to pieces; learn that it is from *de* and *salto*, 'to leap from one thing to another,' as a man who in the ring, technically called a 'desultor,' riding two or three horses at once, leaps from one to the other, being never on the back of any one of them long; take, I say, the word thus to pieces, and put it together again, and what a firm and vigorous grasp will you have now of its meaning! A 'desultory' man is one who jumps from one study to another, and never continues for any length of time in one. Again, you speak of a person as 'capricious,' or as full of 'caprices.' But what exactly are caprices? 'Caprice' is from *capra*, 'a goat.' If ever you have watched a goat, you will have observed how sudden, how unexpected, how unaccountable, are the leaps and springs, now forward, now sideward, now upward, in which it indulges. A 'caprice' then is a movement of the mind as unaccountable, as little to be calculated on beforehand, as the springs and bounds of a goat. Is not the word so understood a far more picturesque one than it was before? and is there not some real gain in the vigour and vividness of impression which is in this way obtained?

The poetry which has been embodied in the names of places, in those names which designate the leading features of outward nature, promontories, mountains, capes, and the like, is very worthy of being elicited and evoked anew, latent as it now has oftentimes become. Nowhere do we so easily forget that names had once a peculiar fitness, which was the occasion of their giving. Colour has often suggested the name, as in the well-known instance of our own 'Albion,'—'the silver-coasted isle,' as Tennyson so beautifully has called it,—which had this name from the white line of cliffs which it presents to those approaching it by the narrow seas. 'Himalaya' is 'the abode of snow.' Often, too, it is shape and configuration which is incorporated in the name, as in 'Trinacria,' or 'the three-promontoried land,' which was the Greek name of Sicily; in 'Drepanum,' or 'the sickle,' the name which a town on the N.W. promontory of the island bore, from the sickle-shaped tongue of land on which it was built. But more striking, as the embodiment of a poetical feeling, is the modern name of the great southern peninsula of Greece. We are all aware that it is called the 'Morea;' but we may not be so well aware from whence that name is derived. It had long been the fashion among ancient geographers to compare the shape of this region to a platane leaf;* and a glance at the map will show that the general outline of that leaf, with its sharply-incised edges, justified the comparison. This, however, had remained merely as a comparison; but at the shifting and changing of names, which went with the breaking up of the old Greek and Roman civilization, the resemblance of this region to a leaf, not now, however, a platane, but a mulberry leaf, appeared so strong, that it exchanged its old name of Peloponnesus for 'Morea,' which embodied men's sense of this resemblance, *morus* being a mulberry tree in Latin, and μορέα in Greek. This etymology of 'Morea' has been called in question;† but on no sufficient grounds. Deducing, as one objector does, 'Morea' from a Slavonic word '*more*,' the sea, he finds in this derivation a support for his favourite notion that the modern population of Greece is not descended from the ancient, but consists in far the larger proportion of intrusive Slavonic tribes.

In other ways also the names of places will oftentimes embody some poetical aspect under which now or at some former period men learned to regard them. Oftentimes when discoverers come upon a new land they will seize with a firm

---

* Strabo, viii. 2; Pliny, *H. N.* iv. 5; Agathemerus, l. i. p. 15; ἔχειν δὲ ὅμοιον σχῆμα φύλλῳ πλατάνου.

† By Fallmerayer, *Gesch. der Halbinsel Morea*, pp. 240 sqq.; and by I. Taylor, *Words and Places*, p. 308.

grasp of the imagination the most striking feature which it presents to their eyes, and permanently embody this in a word. Thus the island of Madeira is now, I believe, nearly bare of wood; but its sides were covered with forests at the time when it was first discovered, and hence the name, 'madeira' in Portuguese having this meaning of wood. Some have said that the first Spanish discoverers of Florida gave it this name from the rich carpeting of flowers which, at the time when first their eyes beheld it, everywhere covered the soil.* Surely Florida, as the name passes under our eye, or from our lips, is something more than it was before, when we may thus think of it as the land of flowers.† We have heard something of Port

---

* But see on this point I. Taylor, *Words and Places*, p. 13.

† An Italian poet, Fazio degli Uberti, tells us that Florence has its appellation from the same cause:

'Poichè era posta in un prato di fiori,
Le denno il nome bello, onde s' ingloria.'

It would be curious, I take the opportunity of observing, to draw together a collection of etymologies which have been woven into verse. These are so little felt to be alien to the spirit of poetry, that on the contrary they exist in large numbers, and often lend to the poem in which they find place a charm and interest of their own. In five lines of *Paradise Lost* Milton introduces four such etymologies, namely, those of the four fabled rivers of hell, though this will no doubt have sometimes escaped the notice of the English reader:

'Abhorred Styx, the flood of deadly *hate*,
Sad Acheron of *sorrow*, black and deep,
Cocytus, named of *lamentation* loud
Heard on the rueful stream; fierce Phlegethon,
Whose waves of torrent *fire* inflame with rage.'

Natal lately, probably we shall in coming years hear still more. The name also embodies an interesting fact, namely that this port was first discovered on Christmas Day, the *dies natalis* of our Lord.

Then again what poetry is there, as indeed there ought to be, in the names of flowers! I do not speak of those, the exquisite grace and beauty of whose names is forced on us so that we cannot miss it, such as 'meadow-sweet,' 'eyebright,' 'sun-dew,' 'forget-me-not,' 'Venus' looking-glass,' 'queen-of-the-meadows,' 'love-in-idleness,' 'reine marguerite,' 'gilt-cup,' a local name for the 'butter-cup,' drawn from the golden gloss of its petals, and the like; but take 'daisy;' surely this charming little English flower, which has stirred the peculiar affection of English poets from Chaucer to Wordsworth, and received the tribute of their song, becomes more charming yet when we know, as Chaucer long ago has told us, that 'daisy' is day's eye, the eye of day; these are his words:

> 'That well by reason it men callen may
> The *daisie*, or else the eye of day.'

For only consider how much is implied here. To the sun in the heavens this name, eye of day, was naturally first given, and those who transferred the title to our little field flower meant no doubt to liken its inner yellow disk or shield to the great golden orb of the sun, and the white florets which encircle this disk to the rays which the sun spreads on all sides around him. What imagination was here, to suggest a comparison such as this, binding together as this does the smallest and the greatest! what a travelling of the poet's eye, with the power which is the privilege of that eye, from earth to heaven, and from heaven to earth, and of linking both together. Call up before your mind's eye the 'lavish gold' of the drooping laburnum when in flower, and you will recognize the poetry of the title, 'the golden rain,' which in German it bears.

And then again, what poetry is there often in the names of birds and beasts and fishes, and indeed of all the animated world around us; how skilfully are these names adapted to bring out the most striking and characteristic features of the object to which they are given. Thus when the Romans became acquainted with the stately giraffe, long concealed from them in the interior deserts of Africa, (which we learn from Pliny they first did in the shows exhibited by Julius Cæsar,) it was happily imagined to designate a creature combining, though with infinitely more grace, yet something of the height and even the proportions of the *camel* with the spotted skin of the *pard*, by a name which should incorporate both these its most prominent features,* calling it the 'camelopard.' Nor can we, I think, hesitate to accept that account as the true one, which describes the

---

* Varro: Quod erat figurâ ut camelus, maculis ut panthera; and Horace (*Ep.* ii. 1, 196):

Diversum confusa genus panthera camelo.

word as no artificial creation of the scientific naturalist, but as bursting extempore from the lips of the populace at the first moment when the novel creature was presented to their gaze. 'Cerf-volant,' a name which the French have so happily given to the horned scarabeus, the same which we somewhat less poetically call the 'stag-beetle,' is another example of what may be effected with the old materials, by merely bringing them into new and happy combinations.

The butterfly is in Spanish 'mariposa.' The derivation is curious, if it may be trusted, and one who has good right to be heard in the matter adduces it with confidence. Nothing in the butterfly is so striking as the alternations of restless movement while it is on the wing, and then of perfect quiet when it has lighted. He divides the word thus, 'mar-i-posa,' or 'sea and rest;' first the restless agitation as of the sea, and this presently exchanged for perfect repose, and finds here a key to the explanation of a word which has hitherto perplexed all etymologists.

You know the appearance of the lizard, and the *star*-like shape of the spots which are sown over its back. Well, in Latin it is called 'stellio,' from *stella*, a star; just as the basilisk had in Greek the name of 'little king' because of the shape as of a *kingly* crown which the spots on its head might be made by the fancy to assume. Need I remind you of our own 'goldfinch,' evidently so called from that bright patch of yellow on its wing; our 'kingfisher,' having its name from the royal beauty, the kingly splendour of the plumage with which it is adorned? The lady-bird or lady-cow is prettily named, as indeed the whole legend about it is full of grace and fancy; but a common name which in many of our country parts it bears, the 'golden knop,' is prettier still.

This word reminds me of the vast amount of curious legendary lore which is everywhere bound up in words, and which they, if duly solicited, will yield back to us again. For example, the Greek 'halcyon,' which we have adopted without change, has reference, and wraps up in itself an allusion, to one of the most beautiful and significant legends of heathen antiquity; according to which the sea preserved a perfect calmness for all the period, the fourteen 'halcyon days,' during which this bird was brooding over her nest. The poetry of the name survives, whether the name suggested the legend, or the legend the name. Take again the names of some of our precious stones, as of the topaz, so called, as some said, because men were only able to *conjecture* (τοπάζειν) the position of the cloud-concealed island from which it was brought.[*]

Very curious is the determination which some words, indeed many, seem to manifest, that their poetry shall not die; or, if it dies in one form, that it shall revive in another. Thus if there is danger that, transferred from one language to another, they shall no longer speak to the imagina-

---

[*] Pliny, *H. N.* xxxvii. 32.

tion of men as they did of old, they will make to themselves a new life, they will acquire a new soul in the room of that which has ceased to quicken and inform them any more. Let me make clear what I mean by one or two examples. The Germans, knowing nothing of carbuncles, had naturally no word of their own for them, and when they first found it necessary to name them, as naturally borrowed the Latin 'carbunculus,' which originally had meant 'a little live coal,' to designate these precious stones of a fiery red. But 'carbunculus,' a real word, full of poetry and life, for a Latin, would have been only an arbitrary sign for as many as were ignorant of that language. What then did they, or what, rather, did the working genius of the language, do? It adopted, but in adopting, modified slightly yet effectually the word, changing it into 'Karfunkel,' thus retaining the outlines of the original, yet at the same time, inasmuch as 'funkeln' signifies 'to sparkle,' reproducing now in an entirely novel manner the image of the bright sparkling of the stone, for every knower of the German tongue.

Take another illustration of this from another quarter. The French 'rossignol,' a nightingale, is undoubtedly the Latin 'lusciniola,' the diminutive of 'luscinia,' with the alteration so frequent in the Romance languages, of the commencing *l* into *r*. Whatever may be the etymology of 'luscinia,' whether it be 'in lucis cano,' the singer in the groves, or 'lugens cano,' the mourning singer, or 'in lucem cano,' the singer until dawn, or, most probably, 'luscus cano,' the weak-eyed and therefore twilight singer, with which our 'nightingale' would most closely correspond, it is plain that for Frenchmen in general the word would no longer suggest any one of these meanings, hardly even for French scholars, after the serious transformations which it had undergone; while yet, at the same time, in the exquisitely musical 'rossignol,' and still more perhaps in the Italian 'usignuolo,' there is an evident intention and endeavour to express something of the music of the bird's song in the liquid melody of the imitative name which it bears; and thus to put a new soul into the word, in lieu of that other which it has let go.

I must add one example more of the dying out of the old life in a word, and the birth of a new in its stead. Every one who has visited Lucerne in Switzerland must remember the rugged mountain called 'Mont de Pilate' or 'Pilate's mountain,' which stands opposite to him; and if he has been among the few who climb it, will have been shown by his guide the lake at its summit in which Pontius Pilate in his despair drowned himself, with an assurance that from this the mountain obtained its name. Nothing of the kind. 'Mont de Pilate' was originally 'Mons *Pileatus*,' 'the *hatted* hill;' the clouds, as one so often sees, gathering round its summit, and forming the shape and appearance of a turban or hat. When in the Middle Ages this true derivation was forgotten or misunderstood, the other was invented and imposed.

An instructive example this, let me observe by the way, of that which has happened continually in far older legends; I mean that the name has suggested the legend, and not the legend the name.

I have said that poetry and imagination seek to penetrate everywhere; and this is literally true; for even the hardest, austerest studies cannot escape their influence; they will put something of their own life into the dry bones of a nomenclature which seems the remotest from them, the most opposed to them. He who in prosody called a metrical foot consisting of one long syllable followed by two short (—◡◡) a 'dactyle' or a finger, with allusion to the long first joint of the finger and the two shorter which follow, whoever he may have been, and some one was the first to do it, must be allowed to have brought a certain amount of imagination into a study so alien to it as prosody very well might appear.

He did the same in another not very poetical region who invented the Latin law-term 'stellionatus.' The word includes all such legally punishable acts of swindling or injurious fraud committed on the property of another as are not specified in any more precise enactment; being drawn and derived from a practice attributed, I suppose without any foundation, to the lizard or 'stellio' we spoke of just now. Having cast its winter skin, it is reported to swallow it at once, and this out of a malignant grudge lest any should profit by that which, if not now, was of old accounted a sure specific in certain diseases. The term was then transferred to any malignant wrong done by one person to another.

In other regions it was only to be expected that we should find poetry. Thus it is nothing strange that architecture, which has been called frozen music, and which is poetry embodied in material forms, should have a language of its own, not dry nor hard, not of the mere intellect alone, but one in the forming of which it is evident that the imaginative faculties were at work. To take only one example—this, however, from Gothic art, which naturally yields the most remarkable—what exquisite poetry in the name of 'the rose window,' or better still, ' the rose,' given to the rich circular aperture of stained glass, with its leaf-like compartments, in the transepts of a Gothic cathedral! Here indeed we may note an exception from that which usually finds place; for usually art borrows beauty from nature, and very faintly, if at all, reflects back beauty upon her. In this present instance, however, art is so beautiful, has reached so glorious and perfect a development, that if the associations which the rose supplies lend to that window some hues of beauty and a glory which otherwise it would not have, the latter abundantly repays the obligation; and even the rose itself may become lovelier still, associated with those shapes of grace, those rich gorgeous tints, and all the religious symbolism of that in art which has borrowed and bears its name. After this it were little to note the imagination, although that was most real, which dictated the term 'flamboyant' to express the wavy flame-like outline, which, at a particular period of art, the tracery in the Gothic window assumed.

'Godsacre,' or 'Godsfield,' is the German name for a burial-ground, and once was our own, though we unfortunately have nearly, if not quite, let it go. What a hope full of immortality does this little word proclaim; how rich is it in all the highest elements of poetry, and of poetry in its noblest alliance, that is, in its alliance with faith —able as it is to cause all loathsome images of decay and dissolution to disappear, not denying them, but suspending, losing, absorbing them in the sublimer thought of the victory over death, of that harvest of life which God shall one day so gloriously reap even there where now seems the very triumphing place of death.

Lastly let me note the pathos of poetry which lies often in the mere tracing of the succession of changes in meaning which certain words have undergone. Thus 'Elend' in German, a beautiful word, now signifies wretchedness, but at first it signified exile or banishment. The sense of this separation from the native land and from all home delights as being the woe of all woes, the crown of all sorrow, little by little so penetrated the word, that what at first expressed only one form of misery, has ended by signifying all. It is not a little notable, as showing the same feeling at work, that 'essil' (= exilium) in old French signified, not as one might have expected, banishment, but ruin.

Let us then acknowledge man a born poet. If not every man always himself a 'maker,' yet evermore able to rejoice in what others have made, adopting it freely, moving gladly in it as his own most congenial element and sphere. For indeed, as man does not live by bread alone, as little does he seek in language merely the instrument which shall put him in such relations with his fellowmen as shall enable him to buy and sell and get gain, or otherwise make provision for the lower necessities of his animal life; but something rather which shall also stand in a real relation and correspondence to the higher faculties of his being, shall feed, nourish, and sustain these, shall stir him with images of beauty and suggestions of greatness. Neither here nor anywhere else could he become the mere utilitarian, even if he would. Despite his utmost efforts, were he mad enough to employ them, he could not succeed in exhausting his language of the poetical element which is inherent in it; he could not succeed in stripping it of blossom, flower, and fruit, and leaving it nothing but a bare and naked stem. He may fancy for a moment that he has succeeded in doing this; but it will only need for him to become a little better philologer, to go a little deeper into the study of the words which he is using, and he will discover that he is as remote from this miserable consummation as ever.

For ourselves, let us desire nothing of the kind.

Our life is not otherwise so full of imagination and poetry that we need give any diligence to empty it of that which it possesses of these. It will always have for us all enough of dull and prosaic and commonplace. What profit can there be in seeking to extend the region of these? Profit there would be none, but on the contrary infinite loss. It is *stagnant* waters which corrupt themselves; not those on which the breath and the winds of heaven are freely blowing. The words of passion and imagination are, as one so grandly called them of old, 'winds of the soul' ($\psi v\chi \hat{\eta}s$ $\overset{\smile}{\alpha}\nu\varepsilon\mu o\iota$), to keep it in healthful motion and agitation, to lift it upward and to drive it onward, to preserve it from that unwholesome stagnation which constitutes the fatal preparedness for so many other and worse evils.

LECTURE III.

ON THE MORALITY IN WORDS.

IS man of a divine birth and stock? coming from God, and, when he fulfils the law of his being, and the intention of his creation, returning to Him again? We need no more than his language to prove it; so much is there in that which could never have existed on any other supposition. How else could all those words which testify of his relation to God, and of his consciousness of this relation, and which ground themselves thereon, have found their way into this, the veritable transcript of his innermost life, the genuine utterance of the faith and hope which is in him? In what other way can we explain that vast and preponderating weight thrown into the scale of goodness and truth, which, despite of all in the other scale, we must thankfully acknowledge that language never is without? How else shall we account for that sympathy with the right, that testimony against the wrong, which, despite of all aberrations and perversions, is yet the prevailing ground-tone of all?

But has man fallen, and deeply fallen, from the heights of his original creation? We need no more than his language to prove it. Like everything else about him, it bears at once the stamp of his greatness and of his degradation, of his glory and of his shame. What dark and sombre threads he must have woven into the tissue of his life, before we could trace those threads of darkness which run through the tissue of his language! What facts of wickedness and woe must have existed in the one, ere such words could exist to designate these as are found in the other! There have never wanted those who would make light of the hurts which man has inflicted on himself, of the sickness with which he is sick; who would persuade themselves and others that moralists and divines, if they have not quite invented, have yet enormously exaggerated, these. But are statements to this effect found only in Scripture and in sermons? Are not mournful corroborations of their truth imprinted deeply upon every province of man's natural and spiritual life, and on none more deeply than on his language? It needs but to open a dictionary, and to cast our eye thoughtfully down a few columns, and we shall find abundant confirmation of this sadder and sterner estimate of man's moral and spiritual condition. How else shall we explain this long catalogue of words, having all to do with sin or with sorrow, or with both? How came they there? We may be quite sure that they were not invented without being needed, and they have each a correlative in the world of realities. I open the first letter of the alphabet; what means this 'Ah,' this 'Alas,' these deep and long-drawn sighs of humanity, which at once encounter me there? And then presently there meet me words such as these, 'Affliction,' 'Agony,' 'Anguish,' 'Assassin,' 'Atheist,' 'Avarice,' and a hundred more—words, you will observe, not laid up in the recesses of the language, to be drawn forth at rare opportunities, but many of them such as must be continually on the lips of men. And indeed, in the matter of abundance, it is sad to note how much richer our vocabularies are in words that set forth sins, than in those that set forth graces. When St. Paul (Gal. v. 19-23) would put these against those, 'the works of the flesh' against 'the fruit of the Spirit,' those are seventeen, these only nine; and where do we find in Scripture such lists of graces, as we do at 2 Tim. iii. 2, Rom. i. 29-31, of their contraries?

Nor can I help noting, in the oversight and muster from this point of view of the words which constitute a language, the manner in which its utmost resources have been taxed to express the infinite varieties, now of human suffering, now of human sin. Thus, what a fearful thing is it that any language should possess a word expressing the pleasure which men feel at the calamities of others; for the existence of the word bears testimony to the existence of the thing. And yet such in more languages than one may be found.* Nor are there want-

---

* In the Greek, ἐπιχαιρεκακία, in the German, 'Schadenfreude.' Cicero so strongly feels the want of such a word that he gives to 'malevolentia' the significance, 'voluptas ex malo alterius,' which lies not of necessity in it.

ing, I suppose, in any language, words which are
the mournful record of the strange wickednesses
which the genius of man, so fertile in evil, has invented.
What whole processes of cruelty are sometimes
wrapped up in a single word! Thus I
hardly open an Italian dictionary before I light
upon the verb 'abbacinare,' meaning to deprive
of sight by holding a red-hot metal basin close to
the eyes. And our dictionaries, while they tell us
much, do not tell us all. How shamefully rich is
everywhere the language of the vulgar in words
and phrases which, seldom allowed to find their
way into books, yet live as a sinful oral tradition
on the lips of men, to set forth that which is unholy
and impure. And of these words, as no less
of those having to do with the kindred sins of revelling
and excess, how many set the evil forth
with an evident sympathy and approbation, as
taking part with the sin against Him who has forbidden
it under pain of his extremest displeasure.
How much cleverness, how much wit, yes, and
how much imagination must have stood in the service
of sin, before it could possess a nomenclature
so rich, so varied, and often so heaven-defying
as it has.

How many words men have dragged downward
with themselves, and made partakers more or less
of their own fall. Having originally an honourable
significance, they have yet with the deterioration
and degeneration of those that used them, or
those about whom they were used, deteriorated
and degenerated too. How many, harmless once,

have assumed a harmful as their secondary meaning; how many worthy have acquired an unworthy. Thus 'knave' meant once no more than lad (nor does it now in German mean more), 'villain' than peasant; a 'boor' was a farmer, a 'varlet' a serving-man, a 'menial' one of the 'many' or household, a 'minion' a favourite (man in Sylvester is 'God's dearest *minion*'); Christ, according to Bishop Hall, was the 'ringleader' of our salvation 'Timeserver,' two hundred years ago quite as often designated one in an honourable as in a dishonourable sense 'serving the time.'* 'Conceits' had once nothing conceited in them. An 'officious' man was one prompt in offices of kindness and not a busy meddler in things that concern him not. 'Demure' conveyed no hint, as it does now, of an overdoing of the outward demonstrations of modesty. In 'crafty' and 'cunning' no crooked wisdom was implied, but only knowledge and skill; 'craft,' indeed, still retains very often its more honourable use, a man's 'craft' being his skill, and then the trade in which he is skilled. Could the Magdalen have ever given us 'maudlin' in its present contemptuous application, if the tears of penitential sorrow had been held in due honour by the world? 'Tinsel,' the French 'étincelle,' meant once anything that sparkled or glistened; thus, 'cloth of *tinsel*' would be cloth inwrought with silver and gold; but the sad experience that 'all is not gold that glitters,' that much which shows fair and specious to the eye is yet worthless in reality, has

---

* See in proof Fuller, *Holy State*, b. 3, c. 19.

caused that by 'tinsel,' literal or figurative, we ever mean now that which has no reality of sterling worth underlying the specious shows which it makes. 'Specious' itself, let me note, meant beautiful at one time, and not as now, presenting a deceitful appearance of beauty. 'Tawdry,' which was applied formerly to lace or other finery bought at the fair of St. Awdrey or St. Etheldreda, has run through the same course: it at one time conveyed no suggestion of *mean* finery, or *shabby* splendour, as now it does. 'Voluble' was an epithet of honour, meaning what 'fluent' means now; 'plausible' was worthy of applause.*

A like deterioration through use may be traced in the verb 'to resent.' Barrow could speak of the good man as a faithful 'resenter' and requiter of benefits, of the duty of testifying an affectionate 'resentment' of our obligations to God. But the memory of benefits fades from us so much more quickly than that of injuries; we remember and revolve in our minds so much more predominantly the wrongs, real or imaginary, men have done us, than the favours we owe them, that 'to resent' has come in our modern English to be confined exclusively to that deep reflective displeasure which men entertain against those that have done, or whom they believe to have done, them a wrong. And this explains how it comes to pass that we do

---

* Having in mind what 'Dirne' means now in German, one almost shrinks from observing that it was once a name of honour which could be and was used of the Blessed Virgin Mary. (See Grimm, *Wörterbuch*, s. v.)

not speak of the 'retaliation' of benefits at all so often as the 'retaliation' of injuries. 'To retaliate' signifies no more than to render again as much as we have received; but this is so much seldomer practised in regard of benefits than of wrongs, that 'retaliation,' though not altogether unused in this worthier sense, has yet, when so employed, an unusual sound in our ears. 'To retaliate' kindnesses is a language which would not now be intelligible to all. 'Animosity,' as originally employed in that later Latin which gave it birth, was spiritedness; men would speak of the 'animosity' or fiery courage of a horse. In our early English it meant nothing more; a divine of the seventeenth century speaks of ' due Christian animosity.' Activity and vigour are still implied in the word; but only as displayed in enmity and hate. There is a Spanish proverb which says, 'One foe is too many; a hundred friends are too few.' The proverb and the course which this word has travelled appear to me mutually to illustrate one another.*

How mournful a witness for the hard and unrighteous judgments we habitually form of one another lies in the word 'prejudice.' It is itself absolutely neutral, meaning no more than a judgment formed beforehand; which judgment may be favourable, or may be unfavourable. Yet so predominantly do we form harsh unfavourable judgments of others before knowledge and experience, that a 'prejudice,' or judgment before knowledge

---

* For quotations from our elder authors in proof of many of the assertions made in the few last pages, see my *Select Glossary*.

and not grounded on evidence, is almost always taken in an ill sense; 'prejudicial' having actually acquired mischievous or injurious for its secondary meaning.

As these words bear testimony to the *sin* of man, so others to his *infirmity*, to the limitation of human faculties and human knowledge, to the truth of the proverb, 'Humanum est errare.' Thus 'to retract' means properly no more than to handle again, to reconsider. And yet, so certain are we to find in a subject which we reconsider, or handle a second time, that which was at the first rashly, imperfectly, inaccurately, stated, which needs therefore to be amended, modified, withdrawn, that 'to retract' could not tarry long in its primary meaning of reconsidering; but has come to signify to withdraw. Thus the greatest Father of the Latin Church, wishing at the close of his life to amend whatever he might then perceive in his various published works incautiously or incorrectly stated, gave to the book in which he carried out this intention (for authors had then no such opportunities as later editions afford now), this very name of '*Retractations*,' being literally 'rehandlings,' but in fact, as will be plain to any one turning to the work, withdrawings of various statements by which he was not any longer prepared to abide.

But urging, as I just now did, the degeneration of words, I should greatly err, if I failed to remind you that a parallel process of purifying and ennobling has also been going forward, most of all through the influences of a Divine faith working in the world. This, as it has turned *men* from evil to good, or has lifted them from a lower earthly goodness to a higher heavenly, so has it in like manner elevated, purified, and ennobled a multitude of the words which they employ, until these, which once expressed only an earthly good, express now a heavenly. The Gospel of Christ, as it is the redemption of man, so is it in a multitude of instances the redemption of his word, freeing it from the bondage of corruption, that it should no longer be subject to vanity, nor stand any more in the service of sin or of the world, but in the service of God and of his truth. The Greek had a word for 'humility;' but for him this humility meant—that is, with rare exceptions—meanness of spirit. He who brought in the Christian grace of humility, did in so doing rescue the term which expressed it for nobler uses and far higher dignity than hitherto it had attained. There were 'angels' before heaven had been opened, but these only earthly messengers; 'martyrs' also, or witnesses, but these not unto blood, nor yet for God's highest truth; 'apostles,' but sent of men; 'evangels,' but not of the kingdom of heaven; 'advocates,' but not 'with the Father.' 'Paradise' was a word common in slightly different forms to almost all the nations of the East; but it was for them only some royal park or garden of delights; till for the Jew it was exalted to signify the wondrous abode of our first parents; and higher honours awaited it still, when on the lips of the Lord, it signified the blissful waiting-place of faithful departed souls (Luke xxiii. 43); yea, the heavenly blessedness itself (Rev. ii. 7). A 'regeneration,' or palingenesy, was not unknown to the Greeks: they could speak of the earth's 'regeneration' in spring-time, of recollection as the 'regeneration' of knowledge; the Jewish historian could describe the return of his countrymen from the Babylonian captivity, and their re-establishment in their own land, as the 'regeneration' of the Jewish State. But still the word, whether as employed by Jew or Greek, was a great way off from that honour reserved for it in the Christian dispensation— namely, that it should be the bearer of one of the most blessed mysteries of the faith. And many other words in like manner there are, 'fetched from the very dregs of paganism,' as Sanderson has it (he instances the Latin 'sacrament,' the Greek 'mystery'), which the Holy Spirit has not refused to employ for the setting forth of the glorious facts of our redemption; and reversing the impious deeds of Belshazzar, who profaned the sacred vessels of God's house to sinful and idolatrous uses (Dan. v. 2), has consecrated the very idol-vessels of Babylon to the service of the sanctuary.

Let us now proceed to contemplate some of the attestations to God's truth, and then some of the playings into the hands of the devil's falsehood, which lurk in words: And first, the attestations to God's truth, the fallings in of our words with his unchangeable Word: for these, as the true uses of the word, while the other are only its abuses, have a prior claim to be considered.

Thus, some modern false prophets, who would gladly explain away all such phenomena of the world around us as declare man to be a sinful being, and lying under the consequences of sin, would fain have us to believe that pain is only a subordinate kind of pleasure, or, at worst, a sort of needful hedge and guardian of pleasure. But a deeper feeling in the universal heart of man bears witness to quite another explanation of the existence of pain in the present economy of the world—namely, that it is the correlative of sin, that it is *punishment*; and to this the word 'pain,' so closely connected with ' 'pœna,' bears witness. Pain *is* punishment; for so the word, and so the conscience of every one that is suffering it, declares. There are those who will not hear of great pestilences being scourges of the sins of men; who, if only they can find out the immediate, imagine that they have found out the ultimate, causes of these; while yet these gainsayers have only to speak of a 'plague,' and they implicitly avouch the very truth which they have set themselves to deny; for a 'plague' what is it but a stroke; so called, because that universal conscience of men which is never at fault, has felt and thus confessed it to be such? For here, as in so many other cases, that proverb stands fast, 'Vox populi, vox Dei;' and may be admitted to the full; that is, if only we keep in mind that this 'people' is not the populace either in high place or in low; and this 'voice of the people' no momentary outcry, but the consenting testimony of the good and wise, of those neither brutalized by ignorance, nor corrupted by a false cultivation, in many places and in many times.

To one who admits the truth of this proverb it will be nothing strange that men should have agreed to call him a 'miser' or miserable, who eagerly scrapes together and painfully hoards the mammon of this world. Here too the moral instinct lying deep in all hearts has borne testimony to the tormenting nature of this vice, to the gnawing pains with which even in this present time it punishes its votaries, to the enmity which there is between it and all joy; and the man who enslaves himself to his money is proclaimed in our very language to be a 'miser,' or miserable man.*

Other words bear testimony to great moral truths. St. James has, I doubt not, been often charged with exaggeration for saying, ' Whosoever shall keep the whole law, and yet offend in one point, he is guilty of all' (ii. 10). The charge is an unjust one. The Romans said as much, as often as they used 'integritas;' we say the same who have adopted 'integrity,' as a part of our ethical language. For what is 'integrity' but entire-

---

* 'Misery' and 'miserable' do not any longer signify avarice and avaricious; but these meanings they also once possessed. (See my *Select Glossary* s. vv.) In them we once said, and in 'miser' we still say, in a word what Seneca when he wrote,— 'Nulla avaritia sine pœnâ est, *quamvis satis sit ipsa pœnarum*,'— took a sentence to say.

ness; the 'integrity' of the body being, as Cicero explains it, the full possession and the perfect soundness of *all* its members; and moral 'integrity,' though it cannot be predicated so absolutely of any sinful child of Adam, is this same entireness or completeness transferred to things higher. 'Integrity' was exactly that which Herod had *not* attained, when at the Baptist's bidding he 'did many things gladly' (Mark vi. 20), but did *not* put away his brother's wife; whose partial obedience therefore profited nothing; he had dropped one link in the golden chain of obedience, and as a consequence the whole chain fell to the ground.

It is very noticeable, and many have noticed, that the Greek word signifying wickedness (πονηρία) comes of another signifying labour (πόνος). How well does this agree with those passages in Scripture which describe sinners as '*wearying themselves* to commit iniquity,' as '*labouring* in the very fire;' 'the martyrs of the devil,' as South calls them, being at more pains to go to hell than the martyrs of God to go to heaven. 'St. Chrysostom's eloquence,' as Bishop Sanderson has observed, 'enlarges itself and triumphs in this argument more frequently than in almost any other; and he clears it often and beyond all exception, both by Scripture and reason, that the life of a wicked or worldly man is a very drudgery infinitely more toilsome, vexatious, and unpleasant than a godly life is.'*

---

* *Sermons*, London, 1671, vol. ii. p. 244.

Take another witness of words to a central truth of our faith. A deep-lying connexion, acknowledged by all, between sin and expiation, a profound conviction that sin requires expiation, cannot be forgiven till an atonement has been made, this, twining itself among the very roots of men's minds, has uttered itself in the words which they employ. No where has it been traced more clearly than in the relation between 'Sünde' and 'sühnen,' the German words for 'sin' and 'to atone.' Some, indeed, have affirmed this relation to be merely fanciful, one, therefore, on which no conclusion could be grounded. But the scholar with best right to speak on the matter, does, after a full discussion, stand fast to this, that the connexion between 'Sünde' and 'sühnen,' though not quite so close as some have assumed, is yet most real; that there thus lies in 'sin' the notion of something needing expiation.* As the great lines in which the human mind travels are still the same, we may recognize as confirming this conclusion the fact that 'piaculum' in the Latin is used for an enormous sin, which, *as such*, demands *expiation*.

How deep an insight into the failings of the human heart lies at the root of many words; and, if only we would attend to them, what valuable warnings many contain against subtle temptations and sins! Thus, all of us have felt the temptation of seeking to please others by an unmanly

---

* Grimm, *Theol. Stud. u. Krit.* 1839, pp. 747 sqq.

assenting to their opinion, even when our own independent convictions did not agree with theirs. The existence of such a temptation, and the fact that too many yield to it, are both declared in the Latin for a flatterer—'assentator'—that is, 'an assenter;' one who has not courage to say *No*, when a *Yes* is expected from him: and quite independently of the Latin, the German, in its contemptuous and precisely equivalent use of 'Jaherr,' a 'yea-Lord,' warns us in like manner against all such unmanly compliances. Let me note that we also once possessed 'assentation' in the sense of unworthy flattering lip-assent; the last example of it in our dictionaries is from Bishop Hall: 'It is a fearful presage of ruin when the prophets conspire in *assentation*.' The word is quite worthy to be revived.

Again, how well it is to have that spirit of depreciation, that eagerness to find spots and stains in the characters of the noblest and the best, who would otherwise oppress and rebuke us with a goodness and a greatness so far surpassing ours,— met and checked by a word at once so expressive, and so little pleasant to take home to ourselves, as the French 'dénigreur,' a 'blackener.' This also has fallen out of use; which is a pity, seeing that the race which it designates is so far from being extinct. Full too of instruction and warning is our present employment of 'libertine.' A 'libertine,' in earlier use, was a speculative free-thinker in matters of religion and in the theory of morals. But as by a sure process free-*thinking* does and will end in free-*acting*, he who has cast off one yoke also casting off the other, so a 'libertine' came in two or three generations to signify a profligate, especially in relation to women, a licentious and debauched person.

Look a little closely at the word 'passion.' We sometimes regard a 'passionate' man as a man of strong will, and of real, though ungoverned, energy. But 'passion' teaches us quite another lesson; for it, as a very solemn use of it declares, means properly 'suffering;' and a 'passionate' man is not one doing something, but one suffering something to be done to him. When then a man or child is 'in a passion,' this is no outcoming in him of a strong will, of a real energy, but the proof rather that, for the time at least, he is altogether wanting in these; he is *suffering*, not doing; suffering his anger, or whatever evil temper it may be, to lord over him without control. Let no one then think of 'passion' as a sign of strength. One might with as much justice conclude a man strong because he was often well beaten; this would prove that a strong man was putting forth his strength on him, but certainly not that he was himself strong. The same sense of 'passion' and feebleness going together, of the first as born of the second, lies, I may remark by the way, in the twofold use of 'impotens' in the Latin, which, meaning first weak, means then violent, and then weak and violent together. For a long time 'impotent' in English embodied the same twofold meaning.

Or meditate on the use of 'humanitas,' and (in Scotland at least) of the 'humanities,' to designate those studies which are esteemed the fittest for training the true humanity in every man. We have happily overlived in England the time when it was still in debate among us whether education were a good thing for every living soul or not; the only question which now seriously divides Englishmen being, in what manner that mental and moral training, which is society's debt to each one of its members, may be most effectually imparted to him. Were it not so, did any affirm still that it was good for any man to be left with powers not called out and faculties untrained, we might appeal to this word 'humanitas,' and the use to which the Roman put it, in proof that he at least was not of this mind, even as now we may not slight the striking witness to the truth herein contained. By 'humanitas' he intended the fullest and most harmonious culture of all the human faculties and powers. Then, and then only, man was truly man, when he received this; in so far as he did not receive this, his 'humanity' was maimed and imperfect; he fell short of his ideal, of that which he was created to be.

In our use of 'talents,' as when we say 'a man of talents' (not 'of talent,' for that, as we shall see presently, is nonsense, though 'of *a* talent' would be allowable), there is a clear recognition of the responsibilities which go along with the possession of intellectual gifts and endowments, whatsoever these may be. We owe our later use of 'talent' to the parable (Matt. xxv. 14), in which talents, more and fewer, are committed to the several servants, that they may trade with them in their master's absence, and give account of their employment at his return. Men may choose to forget the ends for which their 'talents' were given them; they may count them merely something which they have gotten;* they may turn them to selfish ends; they may glorify themselves in them, instead of glorifying the Giver; they may practically deny that they were given at all; yet in this word, till they can rid their vocabulary of it, abides a continual memento that they were so given, or rather lent, and that each man shall have to render an account of their use.

Again, in 'oblige' and 'obligation,' as when we speak of 'being obliged,' or of having 'received an obligation,' a moral truth is asserted—this namely, that having received a benefit or a favour at the hands of another, we are thereby morally *bound* to show ourselves grateful for the same. We cannot prove otherwise without denying not merely a moral truth, but one incorporated in the very language which we employ. Thus South, in a sermon, *Of the odious Sin of Ingratitude*, has well asked, 'If the conferring of a kindness did not *bind* the person upon whom it was conferred to the returns of gratitude, why,

---

* An ἕξις, as the heathen did, not a δώρημα, as the Christian does: see a remarkable passage in Bishop Andrews' *Sermons*, vol. iii. p. 384.

in the universal dialect of the world, are kindnesses still called *obligations* ?' *

Once more—the habit of calling a woman's chastity her 'virtue' is significant. I will not deny that it may spring in part from a tendency, which often meets us in language, to narrow the whole circle of virtues to some one upon which peculiar stress is laid; but still, in selecting this peculiar one as *the* 'virtue' of woman, there speaks out a true sense that this is indeed for her the citadel of the whole moral being, the overthrow of which is for her the overthrow of all; that it is the keystone of the arch, which being withdrawn, the whole collapses and falls.

Or consider all which is witnessed for us in 'kind.' We speak of a 'kind' person, and we speak of man-'kind,' and perhaps, if we think about the matter at all, fancy that we are using quite different words, or the same word in senses quite unconnected. But they are connected, and by closest bonds; a 'kind' person is a 'kinned' person, one of kin; one who acknowledges his kinship with other men, and acts upon it; confesses that he owes to them, as of one blood with himself, the debt of love. And so man*kind* is man*kinned*.† Beautiful before, how much more beautiful do 'kind' and 'kindness' appear, when we apprehend the root out of which they grow;

---

* *Sermons*, London, 1737, vol. i. p. 407.

† Thus Hamlet does much more than merely play on words when he calls his father's brother, who had married his mother, 'A little more than *kin*, and less than *kind*.'

and the truth which they embody; that they are the acknowledgment in loving deeds of our kinship with our brethren; of the relationship which exists between all the members of the human family, and of the obligations growing out of this.

But I said just now that there are also words bearing on them the slime of the serpent's trail; uses, too, of words which imply moral perversity —not upon their parts who employ them now in their acquired senses, but on theirs from whom little by little they received their deflection, and were warped from their original rectitude. A 'prude' is now a woman with an over-scrupulous affectation of a modesty which she does not really feel, and betraying the absence of the substance by this over-preciseness and niceness about the shadow. Goodness must have gone strangely out of fashion, the corruption of manners must have been profound, before matters could have come to this point. 'Prude,' a French word, means properly virtuous or prudent; 'prud'homme' a man of courage and probity. But where morals are greatly and generally relaxed, virtue is treated as hypocrisy; and thus, in a dissolute age, and one incredulous of any inward purity, the 'prude' or virtuous was a sort of female Tartuffe, affecting a virtue which it was taken for granted none could really possess; and the word abides, a proof of the world's disbelief in the realities of goodness, of its resolution to treat them as hypocrisies and shows.

Again, why should 'simple' be used slightingly,

and 'simpleton' more slightingly still? The 'simple' is one properly of a single fold;* a Nathanael, whom as such Christ honoured to the highest (John i. 47); and, indeed, what honour can be higher than to have nothing *double* about us, to be without *duplicities* or folds? Even the world, which despises 'simplicity,' does not profess to admire 'duplicity,' or double-foldedness. But inasmuch as it is felt that a man like this will in a world like ours make himself a prey, and as most men, if obliged to choose between deceiving and being deceived, would choose the former, it has come to pass that 'simple,' which in a kingdom of righteousness would be a word of highest honour, carries with it in this world of ours something of contempt.† Nor can we help noting another involuntary testimony borne by human language to human sin, I mean this,—that an idiot, or one otherwise deficient in intellect, is called an 'innocent,' or one who does no hurt; this use of 'innocent' assuming that to do hurt and harm is the chief employment to which men turn their intellectual powers, that where they are wise, they are oftenest wise to do evil.

Nor are these isolated examples of the contemptuous employment of words expressive of

---

* We must find in it, not 'sine plicâ,' but 'semel plico' (see Donaldson, *Varronianus*, p. 390).

† 'Schlecht' which in modern German means bad, good for nothing, once meant good, good, that is, in the sense of right or strait, but passed very much through the same stages to the meaning which it now possesses, 'albern' in like manner.

goodness. Such meet us on every side. Our
'silly' is the Anglo-Saxon 'sælig,' or blessed. We
see it in a transition state in our early poets, with
whom 'silly' is an affectionate epithet which
sheep obtain for their harmlessness. One among
our earliest calls the new-born Lord of Glory
Himself, 'this harmless *silly* babe.' But 'silly'
has gone through the same process as 'simple,'
'innocent,' and so many more. The same moral
phenomenon repeats itself continually. Thus,
at the first promulgation of the Christian faith,
while the name of its Divine Founder was still
strange to the ears of the heathen, they were
wont, some out of ignorance, but more of intention, slightly to mispronounce this name, turning
'Christus' into 'Chrestus'—that is, the benevolent
or benign. That they who intentionally did this
meant no honour thereby to the Lord of Life, but
the contrary, is certain; and indeed this word
like the 'silly,' 'innocent,' 'simple,' had already
contracted a slight tinge of contempt, or else
there would have been no inducement to fasten it
on the Saviour. What a strange perversion of
the moral sense when a name implying benignity
and goodness had about it an undertone of contempt! The French have their 'bonhommie'
with the same undertone of contempt, the Greeks
also a well-known word. The same moral phenomenon reappears in other quarters. Lady Sheil
tells us of the Persians of this day, 'They have
odd names for describing the moral qualities;
'Sedākat' means sincerity, honesty, candour; but

when a man is said to be possessed of 'sedâkat,' the meaning is that he is a credulous, contemptible simpleton.'* It is to the honour of the Latin, and very characteristic of the best side of Roman life, that 'simplex' and 'simplicitas' never acquired this abusive signification.

Again, how prone are we all to ascribe to chance or fortune those gifts and blessings which indeed come directly from God—to build altars to Fortune rather than to Him who is the author of every good thing. And this faith of men, that their blessings, even their highest, come to them by a blind chance, they have incorporated in a word; for 'happy' and 'happiness' are connected with 'hap,' which is chance;—how unworthy, then, to express any true felicity, whose very essence is that it excludes hap or chance, that the world neither gave nor can take it away.† Against a similar misuse of 'fortunate,' 'unfortunate,' Wordsworth very nobly protests, when, of one who, having lost everything else, had yet kept the truth, he exclaims:

> 'Call not the royal Swede *unfortunate*,
> Who never did to *fortune* bend the knee.'

There are words which reveal a wrong or insufficient aspect which men take of their duties, or which at all events others have taken before them; for it is possible that the mischief may have been done long ago, and those who now use

---

* *Life and Manners in Persia*, p. 247.

† The heathen, with their εὐδαιμονία, inadequate as this word must be allowed to be, put *us* here to shame.

the words may only have inherited it from others, not helped to bring it about themselves. An employer of labour advertises that he wants so many 'hands;' but this language never could have become current, a man could never have thus shrunk into a 'hand' in the eyes of his fellow-man, unless this latter had in good part forgotten that, annexed to those hands which he would purchase to toil for him, were also heads and hearts*—a fact, by the way, of which, if he persists in forgetting it, he may be reminded in very unwelcome ways at the last. In Scripture there is another not unfrequent putting of a part for the whole, as when it is said, 'The same day there were added unto them about three thousand *souls*' (Acts ii. 41). 'Hands' here, 'souls' there—the contrast may suggest some profitable reflections.

There is another way in which the immorality of words mainly displays itself, and in which they work their worst mischief; that is, when honourable names are given to dishonourable things, when sin is made plausible; arrayed, it may be, in the very colours of goodness, or, if not so, yet in such as go far to conceal its own native deformity. 'The tongue,' as St. James has said, 'is *a world* of iniquity' (iii. 6); or, as some would render his words, and they are then still more to our purpose, '*the ornament* of iniquity,' that which sets it out in fair and attractive colours. I

---

* The use of σώματα for slaves in Greek (Rev. xviii. 13) rested originally on the same forgetfulness of the moral worth of every man.

do not believe that these last-named expositors are right, though it is possible to find such a meaning in his words; at the same time the connexion of the Greek for tongue with our 'gloze,' 'glossy,' with the German 'gleissen,' to smooth over or polish, and with an obsolete Greek word signifying the same, is not accidental, but real; even as it points to uses whereunto we may turn this '*best*,' but, as it would then prove, this *worst* 'member that we have.'

How much wholesomer on all accounts is it that there should be an ugly word for an ugly thing, one involving moral condemnation and disgust, even at the expense of a little coarseness, rather than one which plays fast and loose with the eternal principles of morality, makes sin plausible, and shifts the divinely reared landmarks of right and wrong, thus bringing the user under the woe of them 'that call evil good, and good evil, that put darkness for light, and light for darkness, that put bitter for sweet, and sweet for bitter' (Isai. v. 20). On this text, and with reference to this very matter, South has written four of his grandest sermons, bearing this striking title, *On the fatal Imposture and Force of Words*. How awful, yea how fearful, is this 'imposture and force' of theirs, leading men captive at will. There is an atmosphere about them which they are evermore diffusing, a savour of life or of death, which we insensibly inhale at each moral breath we draw.* 'Winds of the soul,' as we

---

* Bacon's words have been often quoted, but they will bear

have already heard them called, they fill its sails, and are continually impelling it upon its course, to heaven or to hell.

Thus how different the light in which we shall have learned to regard a sin, according as we have been wont to designate it, and to hear it designated, by a word which brings out its loathsomeness and deformity; or by one which palliates these and conceals; men, as one said of old, being wont for the most part to be ashamed not of base deeds but of base names. Words of this kind are only too frequent; as when in Italy, during the period when poisoning was rifest, nobody was said to be poisoned; it was only that the death of some was 'assisted' (aiutata). Worse still are words which seek to turn the point of the divine threatenings against some sin by a jest; as when in France a subtle poison, by which impatient heirs delivered themselves from those who stood between them and the inheritance which they coveted, was called 'poudre de succession.' We might suppose beforehand that such clokes for sin would be only found among people in an advanced state of artificial cultivation. But it is not so. Captain Erskine, who visited not many years since in an English ship-of-war the Feijee Islands, and who gives some extraordinary details of the extent to which cannibalism then prevailed

---

being quoted once more: Credunt enim homines rationem suam verbis imponere. Sed fit etiam ut verba vim suam super intellectum retorqueant et reflectant.

among their inhabitants, pork and human flesh being their two staple articles of food, relates in his deeply interesting record of his voyage that natural pig they called '*short* pig,' and man dressed and prepared for food, '*long* pig.' There was doubtless an attempt here to carry off with a jest the revolting character of the practice in which they indulged. For that they were themselves aware of this, that their consciences did bear witness against it, was attested by their uniform desire to conceal, if possible, all traces of the practice from European eyes.

But worst, perhaps, of all are names which throw a flimsy veil of sentiment over some sin. What a source, for example, of mischief without end in our country parishes is the one practice of calling a child born out of wedlock a 'love-child,' instead of a bastard. It would be hard to estimate how much it has lowered the tone and standard of morality among us; or for how many young women it may have helped to make the downward way more sloping still. How vigorously ought we to oppose ourselves to all such immoralities of language; which opposition will yet never be easy or pleasant; for many that will endure to commit a sin, will profoundly resent having that sin called by its right name; like Nym in Shakespeare, whose stealing is not stealing, but 'conveying' ('*convey* the wise it call'); like the electors in some of our corrupter boroughs, who receive, not bribes—they are most indignant if this is imputed to them—but 'head-money' for their votes.'

Coarse as, according to our present usages of language, may be esteemed the words by which our plain-speaking Anglo-Saxon fathers were wont to designate the unhappy women who make a trade of selling their bodies to the lusts of men, yet how much better the truth which is in them than the falsehood of many other titles by which they have been known—names which may themselves be called 'whited sepulchres,' fair without, yet hiding so much foul within; as, for instance, that in the French language which ascribes *joy* to a life which more surely than any other dries up all the sources of gladness in the heart, brings anguish, astonishment, blackest melancholy on all who have addicted themselves to it. In the same way how much more moral words are the English 'sharper' and 'blackleg' than the French 'chevalier d'industrie:'* and the same holds good of the English equivalent, coarse as it is, for the Latin 'conciliatrix.' In this last word we have a notable example of the putting of sweet for bitter, of the attempt to present a disgraceful occupation on an amiable, almost a sentimental side, rather than in its own proper deformity and ugliness.†

---

* For the rise of this phrase see Lemontey, *Louis XIV.* p. 43.

† This tendency of men to throw the mantle of an honourable word over a dishonourable thing, or vice versâ, to degrade an honourable thing, when they do not love it, by a dishonourable appellation, has in Greek a word to describe it, ὑποκορίζεσθαι,

Use and custom soon dim our eyes in such matters as these; else we should be deeply struck by a familiar instance of this falsehood in names, one which perhaps has never struck us at all—I mean the profane appropriation of 'eau de vie' (water of life), a name borrowed from some of the Saviour's most precious promises (John iv. 14; Rev. xxii. 17), to a drink which the untutored savage with a truer instinct has named 'fire-water;' which, sad to say, is known in Tahiti as 'British water;' and which has proved for thousands and tens of thousands, in every clime, not 'water of life,' but the fruitful source of disease, crime, and madness, bringing forth first these, and when these are finished, bringing forth death. There is a blasphemous irony in this appropriation of the language of heaven to that which, not indeed in its use, but too frequent abuse, is the instrument of hell, that is almost without a parallel.*

---

itself a word with an interesting history; while the great ethical teachers of Greece frequently occupy themselves in detecting and denouncing this most mischievous among all the impostures of words. Thus, when Thucydides (iii. 82) would paint the fearful moral ruin which her great Civil War had wrought, he adduces this alteration of the received value of words, this fitting of false names to everything—names of honour to the base, and of baseness to the honourable—as one of its most striking signs; even as it again set forward the evil, of which it had been first the result.

* Milton in a profoundly interesting letter, addressed by him to one of the friends whom he made during his Italian tour, encourages him in those philological studies to which he had devoted his life by such words as these: Neque enim qui sermo,

If I wanted any further evidence of this, the moral atmosphere which words diffuse, I would ask you to observe how the first thing men do, when engaged in controversy with others, be it in the conflict of the tongue or the pen, or of weapons more wounding yet, if such there be, is ever to assume some honourable name to themselves, such as, if possible, begs the whole matter in dispute, and at the same time to affix on their adversaries a name which shall place them in a ridiculous or contemptible, an invidious or odious light.* There is a deep instinct in men, deeper perhaps than they give any account of to themselves, which tells them how far this will go; that multitudes, utterly unable to weigh the arguments of the case, will yet be receptive of the influences which these words are evermore, however imperceptibly, diffusing. By arguments they might hope to gain over the reason of a few, but by help of these nicknames they enlist what at first are so

---

purusne an corruptus, quævo loquendi proprietas quotidiana populo sit, parvi interesse arbitrandum est, quæ res Athenis non semel saluti fuit; immo vero, quod Platonis sententia est, immutato vestiendi more habituque graves in Republicâ motus mutationesque portendi, equidem potius collabente in vitium atque errorem loquendi usu occasum ejus urbis remque humilem et obscuram subsequi crediderim: verba enim partim inscita et putida, partim mendosa et perperam prolata, quid si ignavos et oscitantes et ad servile quidvis jam olim paratos incolarum animos haud levi indicio declarant? Contra nullum unquam audivimus imperium, nullam civitatem non mediocriter saltem floruisse, quamdiu linguæ sua gratia, suusque cultus constitit. Compare an interesting epistle (the 114th) of Seneca.

* See p. 28.

much more effectual, the passions and prejudices of the many, on their side. Thus when at the breaking out of our Civil War the Parliamentary party styled *themselves* 'the Godly,' and the Royalists 'the Malignants,' it is certain that, wherever they could procure entrance for these words, the question upon whose side the right lay was already decided. The Royalists, on the other hand, made exactly the same employment of question-begging words, of words steeped quite as deeply in the passions which animated *them*.

Seeing then that language contains so faithful a record of the good and of the evil which in time past have been working in the minds and hearts of men, we shall not err, regarding it as a moral barometer which indicates and permanently marks the rise or fall of a nation's life. To study a people's language will be to study *them*, and to study them at best advantage; there, where they present themselves to us under fewest disguises, most nearly as they are. Too many have had a hand in language, and in bringing it to its present shape, it is too entirely the collective work of the whole nation, the result of the united contributions of all, it obeys too immutable laws, to allow any successful tampering with it, any making of it to witness other than the actual facts of the case.

Thus the frivolity of an age or nation, its mockery of itself, its inability to comprehend the true dignity and meaning of life, the feebleness of its moral indignation against evil, all this will find an utterance in the employment of solemn and

earnest words in senses comparatively trivial or
even ridiculous. 'Gehenna,' that word of such terrible significance on the lips of our Lord, has in
French issued in 'gêne,' and signifies no more
than a slight and petty inconvenience. 'Honnêteté,'
which should mean that virtue of all virtues, honesty, and which did mean it once, standing as it
does now for external civility and for nothing more,
marks a willingness to accept the slighter observances and pleasant courtesies of society in the
room of deeper moral qualities. Neither is it well
that words, which should have been reserved for the
highest mysteries of the spiritual life, should be
squandered on slight and secular objects,—'spirituel' itself is an example in point,—or that words
implying once the deepest moral guilt, as is the
case with 'perfide,' 'malice,' 'malin' in French,
should be employed now almost in honour, or at
all events in jest and in play.

Often a people's use of some single word will
afford us a deeper insight into their real condition,
their habits of thought and feeling, than whole
volumes written expressly with the intention of
imparting this insight. Thus 'idiot,' a Greek word,
is abundantly characteristic of Greek life. The
'idiot,' or ἰδιώτης, was originally the *private* man,
as contradistinguished from one clothed with office,
and taking his share in the management of public
affairs. In this its primary use it is occasionally
employed in English; as when Jeremy Taylor
says, 'Humility is a duty in great ones, as well as
in *idiots*.' It came then to signify a rude, igno-

rant, unskilled, intellectually unexercised person, a boor; this derived or secondary sense bearing witness to a conviction woven deep into the Greek mind of the indispensableness of public life, even to the right development of the intellect,* a conviction which could scarcely have uttered itself with greater clearness than it does in this secondary use of 'idiot.' Our tertiary, in which the 'idiot' is one deficient in intellect, not merely with its powers unexercised, is but this secondary pushed a little further.—Again, the innermost distinctions between the Greek mind and the Hebrew reveal themselves in the several salutations of each, in the 'Rejoice' of the first, as contrasted with the 'Peace' of the second. The clear, cheerful, world-enjoying temper of the Greek embodies itself in the first; he could desire nothing better or higher for himself, nor wish it for his friend, than to have *joy* in his life. But the Hebrew had a deeper longing within him, and one which finds utterance in his 'Peace.' It is not hard to perceive why this latter people should have been chosen as the first bearers of that truth which indeed enables truly to *rejoice*, but only through first bringing *peace*; nor why from them the word of life should first go forth. It may be urged, indeed, that these were only forms, and such they may have at length become; as in our 'good-by' or 'adieu' we can hardly be said now to commit our friend to the Divine protection; yet still they were not such at

---

* Hare, *Mission of the Comforter*, p. 552.

the first, nor would they have held their ground,
if ever they had become such altogether.

The modifications of meaning which a word has
undergone, as it had been transplanted from one
soil to another, so that one nation borrowing it
from another, has brought into it some force foreign to it before, has deepened, or extenuated, or
otherwise altered its meaning,—this may reveal to
us, as perhaps nothing else would, fundamental
diversities of character existing between them.
The word in Greek exactly corresponding to our
'self-sufficient' is one of honour, and was applied
to men in their praise. And indeed it was the
glory of the heathen philosophy to teach man to
find his resources in his own bosom, to be thus sufficient for himself; and seeing that a true centre
without him and above him, a centre in God,
had not been revealed to him, it was no shame for
him to seek it there; far better this than to have
no centre at all. But the Gospel has taught us
another lesson, to find our sufficiency in God: and
thus 'self-sufficient,' to the Greek suggesting no
lack of modesty, of humility, or of any good thing,
at once suggests such to us. 'Self-sufficiency' no
man desires now to be attributed to him. The
word carries for us its own condemnation; and its
different uses, for honour once, for reproach now,
do in fact ground themselves on the innermost
differences between the religious condition of the
world before Christ and after.

It was not well with Italy, she might fill the
world with exquisite specimens of her skill in the

arts, with pictures and statues of rarest loveliness, but all higher national life was wanting to her, during those centuries in which she degraded 'virtuoso,' or the virtuous man, to signify one accomplished in painting, music, and sculpture; for these, the ornamental fringe of a nation's life, can never, without loss of all manliness of character, be its main texture and woof— not to say that excellence in them has been too often disjoined from all true virtue and worth. The opposite exaggeration of the Romans, for whom 'virtus' meant warlike courage, and the only 'manliness' which they knew, was more tolerable than this; for there is a sense in which a man's 'valour' *is* his value, is the measure of his worth; seeing that no virtue can exist unless men have learned, in Milton's glorious phrase, 'to hate the cowardice of doing wrong.'* It could not but be morally ill with a people among whom 'morbidezza' could be used as a word of praise, expressive of a beauty which claimed for this its 'sickly softness' to be admired. There was too sure a witness here for the decay of moral strength and health, when these could not merely be disconnected from beauty, but implicitly put in opposition to it? How little, again, the Italians, until quite later years, can have lived in the spirit of their ancient worthies, or reverenced the greatest among them, we argue from the fact that

---

* It did not escape Plutarch, poor Latin scholar as he was, that 'virtus' had far more the sense of ἀνδρεία than of ἀρετή (*Coriol.* 1).

they should have been content so far to degrade
the name of one among their noblest, that every
glib and loquacious hireling who shows strangers
about their picture-galleries, palaces, and ruins, is
called 'Cicerone,' or a Cicero! It is unfortunate
that terms like these, having once grown up, are not
again, or are not easily again, got rid of. They
remain, long after the temper that produced them
has passed away.

Happily it is nearly impossible for us in England to understand the mingled scorn, hatred,
fear, suspicion, contempt, which in time past were
associated with the word 'sbirri' in Italian.
These 'sbirri' were the humble, but with this the
acknowledged, ministers of justice; while yet
everything which is mean and false and oppressive, which can make the name of justice hateful,
was implied in this title of theirs. There is no
surer sign of a bad oppressive rule, than when the
titles of the administrators of law, titles which
should be in themselves so honourable, thus
acquire a hateful undertone. What a world of
oppression, chicane, and fraud must have found
place, before tax-gatherer, or exciseman, could be a
word steeped in uttermost scorn, as for the Greek
alike and the Jew it was; while, on the other
hand, however unwelcome the visits of the one or
the interference of the other may be to us, yet the
sense of the entire fairness and justice with which
their offices are fulfilled, acquits these names for
us of the slightest sense of dishonour. 'Police-
man' has no evil sub-audition with us; though in

the last century, when our police was otherwise administered than now, 'catchpole,' in Wiclif's time quite an honourable word, had acquired one. So too, if at this day any accidental profits fall or escheat to the Crown, they are levied so honourably, with such fairness and more than fairness to the subject, that, were not the thing already done, 'escheat' would never yield 'cheat,' nor 'escheator' 'cheater,' as, through the extortions and injustices of which these dues were formerly an excuse, they now have done.

It is worse, as marking that a still holier sanctuary than that of civil government has become profane and contemptible in men's sight, when words which express sacred functions and offices become redolent of scorn. How thankful we may be that in England we have no equivalent to the German 'Pfaffe,' which, the same as 'papa' and 'pope,' and meaning at first but a priest, now carries with it the insinuation of almost every unworthiness in the forms of servility and avarice which can render the priest's office and person base and contemptible.

How much may be learned by noting the words which nations have been obliged to borrow from other nations, as not having them of home-growth —this in most cases, if not in all, testifying that the thing itself was not native, was only an exotic, transplanted, like the word which indicated it, from a foreign soil. Thus it is singularly characteristic of the social and political life of England, as distinguished from that of the other

European nations, that to it alone the word 'club' belongs; France and Germany having been alike unable to grow a word of their own, have borrowed ours. That England should have been the birthplace of the word is nothing wonderful; for these voluntary associations of men for the furthering of such social or political ends as are near to the hearts of the associates could have only had their rise under such favourable circumstances as ours. In no country where there was not extreme personal freedom could they have sprung up; and as little in any where men did not know how to use this freedom with moderation and self-restraint, could they long have been endured. It was comparatively easy to adopt the word; but the ill success of the 'club' itself everywhere save here where it is native, has shown that it was not so easy to transplant the thing. While we have lent this and other words, political and industrial for the most part, to the French and Germans, it would not be less instructive, were this a suitable opportunity, to trace our corresponding obligations to them.

And scarcely less significant and instructive than the presence of a word in a language, will be occasionally its absence. How curious, for instance, are the conclusions which Cicero in his high Roman fashion draws from the absence of any word in the Greek corresponding to the Latin 'ineptus;' not from this concluding, as we might have anticipated, that the character designated by the word was wanting, but rather that the fault was so common, so universal with the Greeks, that they failed to recognize it as a fault at all.*

But it is time to bring this lecture to an end. These illustrations, to which it would be easy to add more, justify our assertion of the existence of a moral element in words; that they do not hold themselves neutral in the great conflict between good and evil, light and darkness, which is dividing the world; that they are not satisfied to be the passive vehicles, now of the truth, and now of falsehood. We see, on the contrary, that they continually take their side, are some of them children of light, others children of this world, or even of darkness; they beat with the pulses of our life; they stir with our passions; they receive from us the impressions of our good and of our evil, which again they are active further to diffuse and to propagate. Must we not own then that there is a wondrous and mysterious world, of which we may hitherto have taken too little account, around us and about us? Is there not something very solemn and very awful in wielding

---

* *De Orat.* ii. 4, 7: Quem enim nos ineptum vocamus, is mihi videtur ab hoc nomen habere ductum, quod non sit aptus. Idque in sermonis nostri consuetudine perlate patet. Nam qui aut tempus quid postulet, non videt, aut plura loquitur, aut se ostentat, aut eorum quibuscum est, vel dignitatis vel commodi rationem non habet, aut denique in aliquo genere aut inconcinnus aut multus est, is ineptus esse dicitur. Hoc vitio cumulata est eruditissima illa Græcorum natio. Itaque quod vim hujus mali Græci non vident, ne nomen quidem ei vitio imposuerunt. Ut enim quæras omnia, quomodo Græci ineptum appellent, non invenies.

such an instrument as this of language is, so mighty to wound or to heal, to kill or to make alive? and may not a deeper meaning than hitherto we have attached to it, lie in that saying, 'By thy words thou shalt be justified, and by thy words thou shalt be condemned'?

LECTURE IV.

ON THE HISTORY IN WORDS.

LANGUAGE, we might not unnaturally suppose, language, that is, as distinct from literature and books, and where these did not exist, would prove the frailest, the most untrustworthy, of all vehicles of the knowledge of the past; that one which would most certainly betray its charge. So far, however, from this being the fact, it is the main, oftentimes the only, connecting link between that past and our present; it is oftentimes an ark riding above the waterfloods that have swept away or submerged every other landmark and memorial of bygone ages and vanished generations of men. Far beyond all written records in a language, the language itself stretches back, and offers itself for our investigation—'the pedigree of nations,' as Johnson calls it—itself a far older and at the same time a far more instructive monument and document than any writing which employs it. The written records may have been falsified by carelessness, by vanity, by fraud, by a multitude of causes; but language is never false, never deceives us, if only we know how to question it aright.

What a voice and testimony it has on a question

perhaps the most deeply interesting of all. Some, as you are aware, on one ground or another deny the accuracy of the Scripture statement that the whole earth was peopled from a single pair; who have sought to establish that there must have been many beginnings, many original centres of human population. Dr. Pritchard and others have shown that Science, quite independent of Revelation, though unable to prove, yet decisively points to, a *physical* unity of the human race. But this is not all. There is much to lead us to anticipate that a stronger evidence and a *moral* argument for the unity of mankind more convincing yet, will some day be forthcoming. We have seen in our own time the consanguinity plainly traced and by all admitted, of families of languages which a very few years ago were esteemed to have absolutely no connection with one another; and while very much remains still to be done, yet assuredly the tendency of all later investigations into languages and their relations, is to refer them more and more to a common stock and single fountain-head.

Such investigations as these, however, lie plainly out of your sphere. Not so, however, those humbler yet not less interesting inquiries, which by the aid of any tolerable dictionary you may carry on into the past history of your own land, as attested by the present language of its people. You know how the geologist is able from the different strata and deposits, primary, secondary, or tertiary, succeeding one another, which he meets, to arrive at a knowledge of the successive physical changes through which a region has passed; is in a condition to preside at those changes, to measure the forces which were at work to produce them, and almost to indicate their date. Now with such a composite language as the English before us, bearing as it does the marks and vestiges of great revolutions profoundly impressed upon it, we may carry on moral and historical researches precisely analogous to his. Here too are strata and deposits, not of gravel and chalk, sandstone and limestone, but of Celtic, Latin, Saxon, Danish, Norman words, and then once more Latin and French, with slighter intrusions from other quarters: and any one with skill to analyse the language might re-create for himself the history of the people speaking that language, might come to appreciate the divers elements out of which that people was composed, in what proportion these were mingled, and in what succession they followed one upon the other.

He would trace, for example, the relation in which the Saxon and Norman occupants of this land stood to one another. An account of this, in the main as accurate as it would be certainly instructive, might be drawn from an intelligent study of the contributions which they have severally made to the English language, as bequeathed to us jointly by them both. Supposing all other records to have perished, we might still work out and almost reconstruct the history by these aids;

even as now, when so many documents, so many institutions survive, this must still be accounted the most important, and that of which the study will introduce us, as no other can, into the innermost heart and life of large periods of our history.

Nor, indeed, is it hard to see why the language must contain such instruction as this, when we a little realize to ourselves the stages by which it has come down to us in its present shape. There was a time when the languages which the Saxon and the Norman severally spoke, existed each by the side of, but unmingled with, the other; one, that of the small dominant class, the other that of the great body of the people. By degrees, however, with the fusion of the two races, the two languages also fused into a third; or rather one prevailed over the other, but only prevailed by receiving a multitude of the words of that other into its own bosom. At once there would exist duplicates for many things. But as in popular speech two words will not long exist side by side to designate the same thing, it became a question how the relative claims of the Saxon and Norman word should adjust themselves, which should remain, which should be dropped; or, if not dropped, should be transferred to some other object, or express some other relation. It is not of course meant that this was ever formally proposed, or as something to be settled by agreement; but practically one was to be taken, one left. Which was it that should maintain its ground? Evidently, where a word was often on the lips of one race, its equivalent seldom on those of the other, where it intimately cohered with the manner of life of one, was only remotely in contact with that of the other, where it laid strong hold on one, and only slight on the other, the issue could not be doubtful. In several cases the matter was simpler still: it was not that one word expelled the other, or that rival claims had to be adjusted; but that there never had existed more than one word, the thing which that word noted having been quite strange to the other section of the nation.

Here is the explanation of the assertion made just now—namely, that we might almost reconstruct our history, so far as it turns upon the Norman conquest, by an analysis of our present language, a mustering of its words in groups, and a close observation of the nature and character of those which the two races have severally contributed to it. Thus we should confidently conclude that the Norman was the ruling race, from the noticeable fact that all the words of dignity, state, honour, and pre-eminence, with one remarkable exception, (to be adduced presently,) descend to us from them—'sovereign,' 'sceptre,' 'throne,' 'realm,' 'royalty,' 'homage,' 'prince,' 'duke,' 'count,' ('earl' indeed is Scandinavian, though he must borrow his 'countess' from the Norman,) 'chancellor,' 'treasurer,' 'palace,' 'castle,' 'hall,' 'dome,' and a multitude more. At the same time the one remarkable exception of 'king' would make us, even did we know nothing of the actual facts, suspect that the chieftain of this ruling race came in not upon a new title, not as overthrowing a former dynasty, but claiming to be in the rightful line of its succession; that the true continuity of the nation had not, in fact any more than in word, been entirely broken, but survived, in due time to assert itself anew.

And yet, while the statelier superstructure of the language, almost all articles of luxury, all having to do with the chase, with chivalry, with personal adornment, is Norman throughout; with the broad basis of the language, and therefore of the life, it is otherwise. The great features of nature, sun, moon, and stars, earth, water, and fire, all the prime social relations, father, mother, husband, wife, son, daughter, these are Saxon. 'Palace' and 'castle' may have reached us from the Norman, but to the Saxon we owe far dearer names, the 'house,' the 'roof,' the 'home,' the 'hearth.' His 'board' too, and often probably it was no more, has a more hospitable sound than the 'table' of his lord. His sturdy arms turn the soil; he is the 'boor,' the 'hind,' the 'churl;' or if his Norman master has a name for him, it is one which on his lips becomes more and more a title of opprobrium and contempt, the 'villain.' The instruments used in cultivating the earth, the 'flail,' the 'plough,' the 'sickle,' the 'spade,' are expressed in his language; so too the main products of the earth, as wheat, rye, oats, bere; and no less the names of domestic animals. Concerning these last it is curious to observe, (and it may be remembered that Wamba, the Saxon jester in *Ivanhoe*, plays the philologer here,)* that the names of almost all animals, so long as they are alive, are thus Saxon, but when dressed and prepared for food become Norman—a fact, indeed, which we might have expected beforehand; for the Saxon hind had the charge and labour of tending and feeding them, but only that they might appear on the table of his Norman lord. Thus 'ox,' 'steer,' 'cow,' are Saxon, but 'beef' Norman; 'calf' is Saxon, but 'veal' Norman; 'sheep' is Saxon, but 'mutton' Norman; so it is severally with 'swine' and 'pork,' 'deer' and 'venison,' 'fowl' and 'pullet.' 'Bacon,' the only flesh which perhaps ever came within his reach, is the single exception.

Putting all this together, with much more of the same kind, which has only been indicated here, we should certainly gather, that while there are manifest tokens preserved in our language, of the Saxon having been for a season an inferior and even an oppressed race, the stable elements of Anglo-Saxon life, however overlaid for a while, had still made good their claim to be the solid groundwork of the after nation as of the after language; and to the justice of this conclusion all other historic records, and the present social condition of England, consent in bearing witness.

But the study of words will throw rays of light upon a past infinitely more remote than this of ours, will reveal to us secrets of the past, which

---

* Wallis, in his *Grammar*, p. 20, had done so before.

else must have been lost to us for ever. Thus it must be a question of profound interest for as many as count the study of man to be far above every other study, to ascertain what point of culture that Indo-European race of which we come, the *stirps generosa et historica* of the world, as one has called it well, had attained, while it was dwelling still as one family in that which was its common home in the East. No voices of history, the very faintest voices of tradition, reach us from ages so far removed from our own. But in the silence of all other voices there is one voice which makes itself heard, and which can tell us much. Where Indian, and Greek, and Latin designate some object by the same word, and where it can be clearly shown that they did not, at a later day, borrow that word one from the other, the object, we may confidently conclude, must have been familiar to the Indo-European race, while yet these several groups of it dwelt as one undivided family together. Now they have such common words for the chief domestic animals, for ox, for sheep, for horse, for dog, for goose, and for many more. From this we have a right to gather that before the migrations began, they had overlived and outgrown the fishing and hunting stages of civilization, and entered on the pastoral. They have *not* all the same words for the main products of the earth, as for corn, wheat, barley, wine; it is tolerably evident therefore that they had not entered on the agricultural stage of existence. So too from the absence of names in common for the principal metals, we have a right to argue that they had not arrived at a knowledge of the working of these. On the other hand, identical names for dress, for house, for numbers as far as a hundred, for the primary relations of the family, for the Godhead, testify that the common stock, intellectual and moral, was not small with which they severally went their way, each to set up for itself and work out its own destinies in its own appointed region of the earth.*

This is one way in which words by their presence or their absence may teach us history which else we could never know. I pass to other ways.

There are vast harvests of historic lore garnered often in single words; important facts which they at once declare and preserve; these too such as sometimes have survived nowhere else but in them. How much history lies in the word 'church.' I see no sufficient reason to dissent from those who derive it from the Greek κυριακή, 'that which pertains to the Lord,' or 'the house which is the Lord's.' A difficulty indeed meets us here. How explain the presence of a Greek word in the vocabulary of our Anglo-Saxon forefathers? for that *we* derive it mediately from them, and not immediately from the Greek, is certain. What contact, direct or indirect, between the languages will account for this? The explanation is curious. While the Anglo-Saxons and

---

* See Mommsen, *Romische Geschichte*, vol. i. c. 2.

IV.   CHURCH, PAGAN.   103

other tribes of the Teutonic stock were almost universally converted through contact with the Latin Church in the western provinces of the Roman Empire, or by its missionaries, some Goths on the Lower Danube had been brought at an earlier date to the knowledge of Christ by Greek missionaries from Constantinople: and this κυριακή, or 'church,' did, with certain other words, pass over from the Greek to the Gothic tongue; and these Goths, the first converted and the first therefore with a Christian vocabulary, lent the word in their turn to the other German tribes, among these to our Anglo-Saxon forefathers; and by this circuit it has come round from Constantinople to us.*

Or again, interrogate 'pagan' and 'paganism,' and you will find important history in them. Many of us are aware that 'pagani,' derived from 'pagus,' a village, had at first no religious significance, but designated the dwellers in hamlets and villages, as distinguished from the inhabitants of towns and cities. It was, indeed, then not unfrequently applied to *all* civilians, as contradistinguished from

---

* The passage most illustrative of the parentage of the word is from Walafrid Strabo (about A.D. 840). Ab ipsis autem Græcis Kyrch à Kyrios, et alia multa accepimus. Sicut domus Dei Basilica, i.e. Regia à Rege, sic etiam Kyrica, i.e. Dominica, à Domino, nuncupatur. Si autem quæritur, quâ occasione ad nos vestigia hæc græcitatis advenerint, dicendum præcipuè à Gothis, qui et Getæ, cùm eo tempore, quo ad fidem Christi perducti sunt, in Græcorum provinciis commorantes, nostrum, i.e. theotiscum sermonem habuerint. Cf. Rudolf von Raumer, *Einwirkung des Christenthums auf die Althochdeutsche Sprache*, p. 288.

the military caste; and this fact may have had a certain influence, when the idea of the faithful as soldiers of Christ was strongly realized in the minds of men. But it was mainly in this way that it became a name for those alien from the faith of Christ. The Church fixed itself first in the seats and centres of intelligence, in the towns and cities of the Roman Empire; in them its earliest triumphs were won; while, long after these had accepted the truth, heathen superstitions and idolatries lingered on in the obscure hamlets and villages; so that 'pagans,' or villagers, came to be applied to *all* the remaining votaries of the old and decaying superstitions, although not all, but only most of them, were such. In an edict of the Emperor Valentinian, of date A.D. 368, 'pagan' first assumes this secondary meaning. We explain 'heathen' in exactly the same way. When the Christian faith was first introduced into Germany, it was the wild dwellers on the heaths who longest resisted the truth. One hardly expects an etymology in *Piers Ploughman*; but this is there:

> '*Hethen* is to mene after heeth,
> And untiled erthe.'

Here, then, are two instructive notices—one, the historic fact that the Church of Christ planted itself first in the haunts of learning and intelligence; another, morally more important, that it shunned not discussion, feared not to encounter the wit and wisdom of this world, or to expose its claims to the searching examination of educated men; but, on the contrary, had its claims first recognized by them, and in the great cities of the world won first a complete triumph over all opposing powers.[a]

I quoted in my first lecture the words of one who, magnifying the advantage to be derived from such studies as ours, observed that oftentimes more might be learned from the history of a word than from the history of a campaign. Words out of number, such as 'sophist,' 'barbarous,' 'clerk,' 'romance,' 'benefice,' 'sacrament,' suggest themselves to me, by aid of any one of which we might prove the truth of the assertion. Let us take 'sacrament;' its history, while it carries us far, will yet carry us by ways full of instruction; and this, while we confine ourselves strictly to this history, not needlessly meddling with discussions about the thing, its place and importance in the Christian scheme. We shall find ourselves first among the forms of Roman law. The 'sacramentum' appears there as the deposit or pledge, which in certain suits plaintiff and defendant were alike bound to make, and whereby they engaged themselves to one another; the loser of the suit forfeiting his pledge to sacred temple uses, from which fact the name 'sacramentum,' or thing consecrated, was first derived.

---

[a] There is a good note on 'pagan' in Gibbon's *Decline and Fall*, c. 21, at the end; and in Grimm's *Deutsche Mythol.* p. 1198; and the history of the changes in the word's use is traced in another interest in Mill's *Logic*, vol. ii. p. 271.

The word, as next employed, plants us amidst the military affairs of Rome, designating the military oath by which the Roman soldiers mutually engaged themselves at the first enlisting never to desert their standards, or turn their backs upon the enemy, or abandon their *Imperator*—this employment teaching us the sacredness which the Romans attached to their military engagements, and going far to account for their victories. The word was then transferred from this military oath to any solemn oath whatsoever. These three stages 'sacramentum' had already passed through, before the Church claimed it for her own, or indeed herself existed at all. Her early writers, out of a sense of the sacredness and solemnity of the oath, transferred this name to almost any act of special solemnity or sanctity, above all to such mysteries as intended more than met eye or ear. For them the Incarnation was a 'sacrament,' the lifting up of the brazen serpent was a 'sacrament,' the giving of the manna, and many things more. It is well to be acquainted with this phase of the word's history, depriving as it does of all convincing power those passages quoted by Romish controversialists from early church-writers in proof of their seven sacraments. It is quite true that these may have called marriage a 'sacrament,' and Confirmation a 'sacrament,' and we may reach the Roman seven without difficulty; but then they called many things more, which even the theologians of Rome do not include in the 'sacraments' properly so called, by the same name; and this

evidence, proving too much, in fact proves nothing
at all. One other stage in the word's history remains; its limitation, namely, to the two 'sacraments,' properly so called, of the Christian Church.
A reminiscence of the employment of 'sacrament,'
an employment which still survived, to signify the
plighted troth of the Roman soldier to his captain
and commander, was that which had most to do
with the transfer of the word to Baptism; wherein
we, with more than one allusion to this oath of
theirs, pledge ourselves to fight manfully under
Christ's banner, and to continue his faithful soldiers
and servants to our life's end; while the *mysterious*
character of the Holy Eucharist was mainly that
which earned for it this name.

We have already found history imbedded in the
word 'frank;' but I must bring forward the Franks
again, to account for the fact with which we are
all familiar, that in the East not Frenchmen alone,
but *all* Europeans, are so called. Why, it may be
asked, should this be? This wide use of 'Frank'
dates from the Crusades; Michaud, the chief
French historian of these, finding evidence here that
his countrymen took a decided lead, as their gallantry well fitted them to do, in these romantic
enterprises of the middle ages; impressed themselves so strongly on the imagination of the East
as *the* crusading nation of Europe, that their name
was extended to all the warriors of Christendom.
He is not here snatching for them more than their
just right. A very large proportion of the noblest
Crusaders, as of others most influential in bringing

these enterprises about, as Peter the Hermit, Pope Urban the Second, St. Bernard, were French, and thus gave, in a way sufficiently easy to explain, an appellation to all.*

To the Crusades also, and to the intense hatred which they roused throughout Christendom against the Mahometan infidels, we owe 'miscreant,' as designating one to whom the vilest principles and practice are ascribed. A 'miscreant,' at the first, meant simply a misbeliever. The name would have been applied as freely, and with as little sense of injustice, to the royal-hearted Saladin as to the vilest wretch that fought in his armies. By degrees, however, those who employed it tinged it more and more with their feeling and passion, more and more lost sight of its primary use, until they used it of any whom they regarded with feelings of abhorrence, resembling those which they entertained for an infidel; just as 'Samaritan' was employed by the Jews simply as a term of reproach, and with no thought whether he on whom it was fastened was in fact one of that detested race or not; where indeed they were quite sure that he was not (John viii. 48). 'Assassin' also, an Arabic word whose story you will find no difficulty in obtaining, belongs to a romantic chapter in the history of the Crusades.†

Various explanations of 'cardinal' have been proposed, which should account for the appropriation of this name to the parochial clergy of the

---
* See Fuller, *Holy War*, b. i. c. 13.
† Gibbon, *Decline and Fall*, c. 64.

city of Rome with the subordinate bishops of that diocese. This appropriation is an outgrowth, and a standing testimony, of the measureless assumptions of the Roman See. One of the favourite comparisons by which that See was wont to set out its relation of superiority to all other Churches of Christendom was this; it was the hinge or 'cardo' on which all the rest of the Church, as the door, at once depended and turned. It followed presently upon this that the clergy of Rome were 'cardinales,' as nearest to, and most closely connected with, him who was thus the hinge or 'cardo' of all.*

'Legend' is a word with an instructive history. We all know what a 'legend' means now. It is a tale which is *not* true, which, however historic in form, is not so in fact, claims no serious belief for itself. It was quite otherwise once. By this name of 'legends' the annual commemorations of the faith and patience of God's saints in persecution and death were originally called; they in this name proclaiming that they were worthy to be read, and from this worthiness deriving their name. At a later day, as corruptions spread through the Church, these 'legends' grew, in Hooker's words, 'to be nothing else but heaps of

---

* Thus a letter professing to be of Pope Anacletus the First in the first century, but really belonging to the ninth: Apostolica Sedos *cardo* et caput omnium Ecclesiarum à Domino est constituta; et sicut *cardine* ostium regitur, sic hujus S. Sedis auctoritate omnes Ecclesiæ reguntur. And we have 'cardinal' put in relation with this 'cardo' in a genuine letter of Pope Leo the Ninth: Clerici summæ Sedis *Cardinales* dicuntur, *cardini* utique illi quo cætera moventur, vicinius adhærentes.

frivolous and scandalous vanities,' having been 'even with disdain thrown out, the very nests which bred them abhorring them.' How steeped in falsehood, to what an extent, according to Luther's indignant turn of the word, the 'legends' (Legende) must have become 'lyings' (Lügende), we can best guess, when we measure the moral forces which must have been at work, before that which was accepted at the first as 'worthy to be read,' should have been felt by this very name to announce itself as most unworthy to be read, to be destitute of all true worth, to belong at best to the region of fable, if not to that of actual untruth.

An inquiry into the pedigree of 'dunce' lays open to us an important page in the intellectual history of Europe. Certain theologians in the middle ages were termed Schoolmen; having been formed and trained in the cloister and cathedral *schools* which Charlemagne and his immediate successors had founded. These were men not to be lightly spoken of, as they often are by those who never read a line of their works, and have not a hundredth part of their wit; who moreover little guess how many of the most familiar words which they employ, or misemploy, have descended to them from these. 'Real,' 'virtual,' 'entity,' 'nonentity,' 'equivocation,' all these, with many more unknown to classical Latin, but now almost necessities to us, were first coined by the Schoolmen; and, passing over from them into the speech of those more or less interested in their speculations, have gradually filtered through the successive strata of society, till now they have reached, some of them, to quite the lowest. At the revival of learning, however, their works fell out of favour: they were not written in classical Latin: the form in which their speculations were thrown was often unattractive; it was mainly in their authority that the Romish Church found support for its perilled dogmas. On all these accounts it was esteemed a mark of intellectual progress to have broken with them, and thrown off their yoke. Some, however, still clung to these Schoolmen, and to one in particular, *Duns* Scotus, the chief teacher of the Franciscan order; and many times an adherent of the old learning would seek to strengthen his position by an appeal to its famous doctor, familiarly called Duns; while those of the new learning would contemptuously rejoin, 'Oh, you are a *Dunsman*,' or more briefly, 'You are a *Duns*,'—or, 'This is a piece of *dunsery*;' and inasmuch as the new learning was ever enlisting more and more of the genius and scholarship of the age on its side, the title became more and more a term of scorn: 'Remember ye not,' says Tyndal, 'how within this thirty years and far less, the old barking curs, *Dunce's* disciples, and like draff called Scotists, the children of darkness, raged in every pulpit against Greek, Latin, and Hebrew?' And thus from that long extinct conflict between the old and the new learning, that strife between the medieval and the modern theology, we inherit 'dunce' and 'duncery.' The lot of Duns was certainly a hard one, who, whatever his merits as a teacher of Christian truth, was assuredly one of the keenest and most subtle-witted of men. He, the 'subtle Doctor' by pre-eminence, for so his admirers called him, 'the wittiest of the school divines,' as Hooker does not scruple to style him, could scarcely have anticipated, and very little deserved, that his name should be turned into a by-word for invincible stupidity.

This is but one example of the singular fortune waiting upon words. We have another of a parallel injustice, in the use which 'mammetry,' a contraction of 'Mahometry,' obtained in our early English. Mahometanism being the most prominent form of false religion with which our ancestors came in contact, 'mammetry' was used, up to and beyond the Reformation, to designate first any false religion, and then the worship of idols; idolatry being proper to, and a leading feature of, most of the false religions of the world. Men did not pause to remember that Mahometanism is the great exception, being as it is a protest against all idol-worship whatsoever; so that it was a signal injustice to call an idol 'a mammet' or a Mahomet, and idolatry 'mammetry.' To pursue the fortunes of the word a little further, at the next step not religious images only, but dolls were called 'mammets;' and when in *Romeo and Juliet* old Capulet contemptuously styles his daughter 'a whining *mammet*,' the process is strange, yet its every step easy to be traced, whereby the name of the Arabian false prophet is fastened on the fair maiden of Verona.

A misnomer such as this may remind us of the immense importance of possessing such names for things as shall not involve or suggest an error. We have already seen this in the province of the moral life; but in other regions also it nearly concerns us. Resuming, as words do, the past, moulding the future, how important it is that significant facts or tendencies in the world's history should have their right names. It is a corrupting of the very springs and sources of knowledge, when we bind up not a truth, but an error, in the very nomenclature which we use. It is the putting of an obstacle which, however imperceptibly, is yet ever at work, hindering any right apprehension of the thing which has been thus erroneously noted.

Out of a sense of this, an eminent German scholar of the last century, writing *On the Influence of Opinions on Words*, did not stop here, nor make this the entire title of his book, but added another and further clause—*and on the Influence of Words on Opinions;** the matter which fulfils the promise of this latter half of the title of his work constituting by far its most interesting and original portion: for while the influence of opinions on words would be called in question by none, sounds like a truism, this, on the contrary,

---

* *Von der Einfluss der Meinungen in die Sprache, und der Sprache in die Meinungen*, von J. D. Michaëlis. Berlin, 1760.

of words on opinions, would doubtless present itself as a novelty to many. And yet it is an influence which has been powerfully felt in every region of human knowledge, in science, in art, in morals, in theology. The reactive energy of words, not merely on the passions of men (for that of course), but on their calmly formed opinions, would furnish a very curious chapter in the history of human knowledge and human ignorance.

Sometimes words with no fault of theirs, for they did not originally bind up any error, will yet draw some error in their train, of which error they will afterwards prove the most effectual bulwark and shield. Let me instance—the author just referred to supplies the example—the word 'crystal.' The strange notion concerning the origin of the thing, current among the natural philosophers of antiquity, and which only two centuries ago Sir Thomas Browne thought it worth while to place first and foremost among the '*Vulgar Errors*' which he undertook to dissipate, was plainly traceable to a confusion occasioned by the name. Crystal, as they supposed, was ice or snow which had undergone such a process of induration, as totally and for ever to have lost its fluidity;* and Pliny, backing up one error by another, affirmed that it was only found in regions of extreme cold. The fact is, that the Greek word for crystal originally signified ice;

---

* Augustine: Quid est crystallum? Nix est glacie durata per multos annos ita ut a sole vel igne facile dissolvi non possit.

but was early transferred to that which so nearly resembles ice as does the diaphanous quartz, which alone *we* call by this name; and then in a little while it was taken for granted that the two, having the same name, were in fact the same substance; and this mistake it took ages to correct.

Natural history abounds with legends. In the word 'leopard' one of these has been permanently bound up; the error, having first given birth to the name, being afterwards itself maintained and propagated by it. The leopard, as is well known, was not for the Greek and Latin zoologists a species by itself, but a mongrel birth of the male panther or pard and the lioness; and in 'leopard or 'lion-pard,' this fabled double descent is expressed.* 'Cockatrice' embodies a somewhat similar fable.

'Gothic' is plainly a misnomer, and has often been a misleader as well, when applied to a style of architecture which belongs not to one, but to all the Germanic tribes; which, moreover, did not come into existence till many centuries after any people called Goths had ceased from the earth. Those, indeed, who first called this medieval architecture 'Gothic,' had no intention of ascribing to the Goths the first invention of it, however this language may seem now to bind up in itself an assertion of the kind. 'Gothic' was at first a mere random name of contempt. The Goths,

---

* This error lasted into modern times; thus Fuller (*A Pisgah Sight of Palestine*, vol. i. p. 195); 'Leopards and mules are properly no creatures.'

with the Vandals, being the standing representatives of the rude in manners and barbarous in taste, they who would throw scorn on this architecture as compared with that classical Italian which alone seemed worthy of their admiration,* called it 'Gothic,' meaning rude and barbarous thereby. We, who recognize in this Gothic the most wondrous and consummate birth of genius in one region of human art, find it hard to believe that this was once a title of scorn, and sometimes erroneously assume some reference here to the people among whom first it arose.

'Classical' and 'romantic,' names given to opposing schools of literature and art, contain an absurd antithesis; and either say nothing at all, or say something erroneous. 'Revival of learning' is a phrase only partially true when applied to that mighty intellectual movement in Western Europe which marked the close of the fifteenth century and the beginning of the sixteenth. A revival there might be, and indeed there was, of *Greek* learning at that time; but there could not be properly affirmed a revival of Latin, inasmuch as it had never been dead; or, if it had, still had revived long before. 'Renaissance,' applied in France to the new direction which art took about

---

* The name, as the designation of a style of architecture, came to us from Italy. Thus Fuller in his *Worthies*: 'Let the Italians deride our English and condemn them for *Gothish* buildings.' See too a very curious expression of men's sentiments about Gothic architecture as simply barbarous, in Phillips's *New World of Words*, 1706, s. v. 'Gothick.'

the age of Francis the First, is another question-begging word. Very many would entirely deny that the bringing back of antique pagan forms into Christian art was a 'renaissance' or new birth of it at all.

But inaccuracy of naming may draw after it more serious mischief in regions more important. Nowhere is accuracy more vital than in words having to do with the great facts and objects of our faith; for such words, as Coleridge has observed, are never inert, but constantly exercise an immense reactive influence on those who employ them, even as they spread around them an atmosphere, which those who often use, or hear them used, unconsciously inhale. The so-called 'Unitarians,' claiming by this name of theirs to be asserters of the unity of the Godhead, claim that which belongs to us by far better right than to them; which, indeed, belonging of fullest right to us, does not properly belong to them at all. I should, therefore, without any intention of offence, refuse the name to them; just as I should decline, by calling those of the Roman obedience 'Catholics,' to give up the whole question at issue between us and them. So, also, did I hold with them, I should never, however convenient it might sometimes be, consent to call the great religious movement of Europe in the sixteenth century the 'Reformation.' Such in our esteem it was, and in the deepest, truest sense of the word; a reforming of things that were amiss in the Church. But how any who esteem it a disastrous, and, on their part who brought it about, a most guilty schism, can call it by this name, is surprising.

Let me urge on you here the importance of seeking in every case to acquaint yourselves with the circumstances under which any body of men who have played an important part in history, above all in the history of your own land, obtained the name by which they were afterwards willing to be known, or which was used for their designation by others. This you may do as a matter of historical inquiry, and keeping entirely aloof in spirit from the scorn, the bitterness, the falsehood, the calumny, out of which very frequently these names were first imposed. Whatever of these may have been at work in them who coined or gave currency to the name, the name itself can never without serious loss be neglected by any who would truly understand the moral significance of the thing; always something, often much, may be learned from it. Learn, then, about each one of these names which you meet in your studies, whether it was one which men gave to themselves; or one imposed on them by others, and which they never recognized; or one which being first imposed by others, was yet in course of time admitted and allowed by themselves. We have examples in all these kinds. Thus the 'Gnostics' called *themselves* such; the name was of their own devising, and declared that whereof they made their boast; it was the same with the 'Cavaliers' of our Civil War. 'Quaker,' 'Puritan,' 'Roundhead,' were all, on the contrary, names devised by others, and never accepted by those to whom they were attached; while 'Whig' and 'Tory' were nicknames originally of bitterest scorn and party hate, given by two political bodies in England to one another,* the Whig being properly a sour Scottish Covenanter, the Tory an Irish bog-trotting freebooter; while yet these nicknames in tract of time so lost and let go what was offensive in them, that in the end they were adopted by the very parties themselves. The German 'Lutherans' were originally so called by their antagonists.† In the same way 'Methodists' was a name not first taken by the followers of Wesley, but fastened on them by others, while yet they have been subsequently willing to accept and to be known by it. 'Capuchin' was a jesting name, given by the boys in the streets to that branch of the Franciscans which afterwards accepted it as their proper designation. It was provoked by the peaked and pointed hood (capucho) which they wore.

A 'Premier' or 'Prime Minister,' though unknown to the law of England, is at present one of the institutions of the country. The acknowledged leadership of one member of the Government is a fact of only gradual growth in our constitutional history, but one in which the nation has entirely acquiesced,—nor is there anything invidious now

---

* In North's *Examen*, p. 321, is a very lively, though not a very impartial, account of the rise of these names.

† Dr. Eck, one of the earliest who wrote against the Reformation, first called the Reformed Lutherani.

in the name. But in what spirit the Parliamentary Opposition, having coined the term, applied it first to Sir Robert Walpole, is plain from some words of his spoken in the House of Commons Feb. 11, 1742: 'Having invested me with a kind of mock dignity, and styled me a *Prime Minister*, they [the Opposition] impute to me an unpardonable abuse of the chimerical authority which they only created and conferred.'

Now of these titles some undoubtedly, like 'capuchin' which I instanced just now, stand in no living connexion with those that bear them; and such, though seldom without their instruction, yet plainly are not so instructive as others, in which the innermost heart of the thing named so utters itself, that, having mastered the name, we have placed ourselves at the central point, from which best to master everything besides. It is thus with 'Gnostic' and 'Gnosticism:' in the prominence given to *gnosis* or knowledge, as opposed to faith, lies the key to the whole system. The Greek Church has loved ever to style itself, the Holy 'Orthodox' Church, the Latin, the Holy 'Catholic' Church. Follow up the thoughts which these words suggest. What a world of teaching they contain; above all when brought into direct comparison and opposition one with the other. How does all which is innermost in the Greek and Roman mind unconsciously reveal itself here; the Greek Church regarding as its chief blazon that its speculation is right, the Latin that its empire is universal. Nor indeed is it merely the

Greek and Latin Churches which utter themselves here, but Greece and Rome in their deepest distinctions, as these existed from the beginning. The key to the whole history, Pagan as well as Christian, of each is in these words. We can understand how the one established a dominion in the region of the mind which shall never be overthrown, the other founded an empire in the world whose visible effects shall never be done away. This is an illustrious example; but I am bold to affirm that, in their degree, all parties, religious and political, which have risen up in England, are known by names that will repay study; by names, to understand which will bring us far to an understanding of their strength and their weakness, their truth and their error, the idea and intention according to which they wrought. 'Puritans,' 'Fifth-Monarchy Men,' 'Seekers,' 'Levellers,' 'Independents,' 'Friends,' 'Rationalists,' 'Latitudinarians,' 'Freethinkers,' these titles, with many more, have each its significance; and would you understand what any of these intended, you must first understand what they were called. From this you must start; even as you must bring back to this whatever further information you may acquire; putting your later gains, if possible, in subordination to the name; at all events in relation and connexion with it.

You will often be able to glean knowledge from the names of things, if not as important as all this, yet interesting in its way. What a record of inventions, how much of the history of commerce, is preserved in names! Thus the 'magnet' has its name from Magnesia; the 'baldachin' from 'Baldacco,' the Italian name of Bagdad; from which city the costly silk which composed this canopy originally came. The 'bayonet' tells us that it was first made at Bayonne—'worsted' that it was first spun at a village so called (in the neighbourhood of Norwich)—'sarsnet' that it is a Saracen manufacture—'cambric' that it reached us from Cambray—'crape' from Cyprus (the earlier form of the word is 'cypres')—'copper' also that it drew its name from this same island, so richly furnished with mines of this metal—'diaper' that it came from Ypres—'damask' from Damascus (the 'damson' also is the 'damascene' or Damascus plum)—'arras' from Arras—'dimity' from Damietta—'gauze' from Gaza—'cordwain' or 'cordovan' from Cordova—'currants' from Corinth—'delf' from Delft—'indigo' (indicum) from India—'gamboge' from Gambodia—'agates' from a Sicilian river, Achates—'jet' from a river Gages in Lycia, where this black stone is found.* 'Rhubarb' is a corruption of Rhu barbarum, the root from the savage banks of the Rhu or Volga—'jalap' is from Xalapa, a town in Mexico—'jane' from Genoa—'parchment' from Pergamum. The 'bezant,' so often named in our early literature, is money of Byzantium; the 'guinea' was originally coined (in 1663)

---

* In Holland's *Pliny*, the Greek form 'gagates' is still retained, though he calls it more commonly 'jeat' or 'goat.'

of gold brought from the African coast so called. The pound or penny 'sterling' was a certain weight of bullion according to the standard of the Esterlings, or Eastern merchants from the Hanse towns on the Baltic. The fashion of the 'cravat' was borrowed from the Croats, or Crabats, as this wild soldiery of the Thirty Years' War used to be called. The 'biggen,' a plain cap often mentioned by our early writers, was first worn by the Beguines, communities of pietist women in the Middle Ages. England now sends her calicoes and muslins to India and the East; yet these words give standing witness that we once imported them from thence; for 'calico' is from Calicut, and 'muslin' from Moussul, a city in Asiatic Turkey. 'Ermine' is the spoil of the Armenian rat; the 'spaniel' is from Spain, or perhaps from Hispaniola; 'Sherry,' or 'Sherris,' as Shakespeare wrote it, is sent us from Xeres; and 'port' from Oporto. The 'pheasant' reached us from the banks of the Phasis; the 'bantam' from a Dutch settlement in Java of the same name; the 'cherry' was brought by Lucullus from Cerasus, a city in Pontus; the 'peach' declares itself a Persian fruit; the 'quince' has undergone so many changes in its progress through Italian and French to us, that it hardly retains any trace of Cydon (malum Cydonium), a town of Crete, from which, however, it is called.

Occasionally a name will embody and give permanence to an error; as when in 'America' the discovery of the New World, which belonged to Columbus, is ascribed to another eminent discoverer; but one who had no title to this honour, and was entirely guiltless of any attempt to usurp it for himself.* Our 'turkeys' are not from Turkey, as their name seems to say, and as was assumed by those who imposed that name, but from that New World where alone they are native. This error the French in another shape repeat, calling it 'dinde,' originally 'poulet d'Inde,' or Indian fowl. There lies in 'gypsy' or Egyptian the assumption that Egypt was the original home of this strange people; as was widely believed when they made their first appearance in Europe early in the fifteenth century. That this, however, was a mistake, their language leaves no doubt; proclaiming as it does that they are wanderers from a more distant East, an outcast tribe from Hindostan. 'Bohemians,' as they are called by the French, testifies to an error of a like character, to the fact that at their first apparition they were supposed by the common people in France to be the expelled Hussites of Bohemia.

Where words have not embodied an error, it will yet sometimes happen that the sound or spelling of a word will *to us* suggest a wrong explanation, against which in these studies it will need to be on our guard. There has been a stage in most boys' geographical knowledge, when they have taken for granted that Jutland was so called, not because it was the land of the Jutes, but on

---

* Humboldt has abundantly shown this (*Cosmos*, vol. ii. note 457). He ascribes its general reception to its introduction into a popular work on geography, published in 1507.

IV. THE PICTS NOT THE PAINTED.

account of its *jutting* out into the sea in so remarkable a manner. As the oak, in Greek δρῦς, plays no inconsiderable part in the religious discipline of the Druids, it is not wonderful if most students at one time of their lives have put the two in etymological connexion. The Greeks, who in so incomprehensible a manner assumed that words in all languages were to be explained by the Greek, did so of course. So, too, there have not been wanting those who have traced in the name 'Jove' a heathen reminiscence of the awful name of Jehovah; while yet, however specious this may seem, on closer scrutiny the words declare that they have no connexion with one another.

Sometimes a falsely-assumed derivation has reacted upon and modified the spelling. Thus the name of the Celtic tribe whom we call the 'Picts,' would not have come down to us exactly in this form, but for the notion which early got abroad, that they were so called from their custom of staining or painting their bodies, that in fact 'Pict' meant 'the painted.' This in itself is most unlikely. We can quite conceive the Romans giving this name to the *first* barbarous people they encountered, who were in the habit of thus painting themselves. For such a custom, forcing itself on the eye, and impressing itself on the imagination, is exactly the motive which gives birth to a name. But *after* they had been long familiar with the tribes in southern Britain, among whom this painting or tattooing was equally in use, it is inconceivable that they should have applied it to a northern tribe, with which they first came in contact at a far later day. The name is more probably the original Celtic one, 'peichta,' or 'The fighters,' slightly modified to give it a Latin shape and sound in the mouths of the Romans. It may have been the same with 'hurricane.' In the tearing up and *hurrying* away of the *canes* in the sugar plantations by this West Indian tornado, many have seen an explanation of the name; just in the same way as the Latin 'calamitas' has been derived from 'calamus,' the stalk of the corn. In both cases the etymology is faulty; 'hurricane,' probably a Carib word at the first, is only a transplanting into our tongue of the Spanish 'hurracan' or the French 'ouragan.'

It is a signal evidence of the conservative powers of language, that we may continually trace in speech the record of customs and states of society which have now passed so entirely away as to survive in these words alone. For example, a 'stipulation' or agreement is so called, as many affirm, from 'stipula,' a straw; and tells of a Roman custom, that when two persons would make a mutual engagement with one another,* they would break a straw between them. We all know what fact of English history is laid up in 'curfew' or 'couvre-feu.' The 'limner,' or 'lumineur' (luminatore), throws us back on a time when the *illumination* of manuscripts was the

---

* See on this disputed point, and on the relation between the Latin 'stipulatio' and the old German custom not altogether dissimilar, J. Grimm, *Deutsche Rechtsalterthümer*, pp. 121, sqq.

leading occupation of the painter; so that from this work he derived his name. 'Thrall' and 'thraldom' descend to us from a period when it was the custom to *thrill* or drill the ear of a slave in token of servitude; a custom in use among the Jews (Deut. xv. 17), and retained by our Anglo-Saxon forefathers, who were wont thus to pierce at the church door the ears of their bond-servants. By 'lumber,' we are, or might be, taught that Lombards were the first pawnbrokers, even as they were the first bankers, in England; a 'lumber'-room being a 'lombard'-room, or a room where the pawnbroker stored his pledges.* Nor need I do more than remind you that in our common phrase of '*signing* our name,' we preserve a record of a time when such first rudiments of education as the power of writing, were the portion of so few, that it was not as now an exception, but the custom, of most persons to make their mark or 'sign;' great barons and kings themselves not being ashamed to set this *sign* or cross to the weightiest documents. To 'subscribe' the name would more accurately express what now we do. As often as we term arithmetic the science of 'calculation,' we allude to that rudimental period of the science of numbers, when pebbles (calculi) were used, as now among savages they often are, to facilitate the practice of counting; the Greeks did the same in a word of theirs ($\psi\eta\phi i\zeta\epsilon\iota\nu$); as in another ($\pi\epsilon\mu\pi\acute{a}\zeta\epsilon\iota\nu$) record of a period was kept when the *five* fingers were so employed. 'Expend,'

---

* See my *Select Glossary* s. v. Lumber.

'expense,' tell us that money was once weighed out (Gen. xxxiii. 16), not counted out as now. In 'library' we preserve the fact that books were written on the bark (liber) of trees; in 'volume' that they were rolls; in 'book' itself that they were beechen tablets; as in 'paper,' that the Egyptian papyrus, 'the paper reeds by the brooks,' furnished at one time the chief material for writing.

Names thus so often surviving things, we have no right to turn an etymology into an argument. There was a notable attempt to do this in the controversy so earnestly carried on between the Greek and Latin Churches about the bread, whether it should be leavened or unleavened, that was used at the Table of the Lord. Those of the Eastern Church constantly urged that the Greek word for bread (and in Greek was the authoritative record of the first institution of the Holy Communion) implied, according to its root, that which was raised or lifted up; not, therefore, to use a modern term, sad or set, that is, unleavened bread, but such rather as had undergone the process of fermentation. But even if the etymology on which they relied (ἄρτος from αἴρω to raise) had been as certain as it is questionable, they could draw no argument of the slightest worth from so remote an etymology, and one which had so long fallen out of the consciousness of those who employed the word.

Theories too, which long since were utterly renounced, have yet left their traces behind them. Thus 'good humour,' 'bad humour,' 'humours,'

and, strangest contradiction of all, '*dry* humour,'
rest altogether on a now exploded, but a very old
and widely extended, theory of medicine; according to which there were four principal moistures or 'humours' in the natural body, on the
due proportion and combination of which the disposition alike of body and of mind depended.* Our
present use of 'temper' has its origin in the same
theory; the due admixture, or right 'tempering,'
of these humours gave what was called the happy
temper, or mixture, which, thus existing inwardly,
manifested itself also outwardly; while 'distemper,' which we still employ in the sense of
sickness, was that evil frame either of a man's
body or of his mind (for it was used of both)
which had its rise in an unsuitable mingling of
these humours. In these instances, as in many
more, the great streams of thought and feeling
have changed their course, flowing now in quite
other channels from those which once they filled,
but have left these words as lasting memorials of
the channels in which once they ran.

Other singular examples we have of the way in
which the record of old errors, themselves dismissed long ago, may yet survive in language,—
being bound up in words, which grew into use
when those errors found credit, and which maintain their currency still. The mythology which
our ancestors brought with them from their Ger-

---

* See the *Prologue* to Ben Jonson's *Every Man out of his Humour*.

man or Scandinavian homes is as much extinct for us as are the Lares, Larvæ, and Lemures of heathen Rome; yet the deposit it has permanently left in that well-stored antiquarian museum, the English language, is not inconsiderable. 'Lubber,' 'dwarf,' 'oaf,' 'droll,' 'wight,' 'urchin,' 'hag,' 'night-mare,' 'grammary,' 'Old Nick,' 'changeling' (wechselkind), 'wicked,' suggest themselves, as all bequeathed to us by that old Gothic demonology. No one now puts any faith in astrology, counts that the planet under which a man is born will affect his temperament, make him for life of a disposition grave or gay, lively or severe. Yet our language affirms as much; for we speak of men as 'jovial,' or 'saturnine,' or 'mercurial'—'jovial,' as being born under the planet Jupiter or Jove, which was the joyfullest star, and of happiest augury of all:* a gloomy severe person is said to be 'saturnine,' born, that is, under the planet Saturn, who makes those that own his influence, being born when he was in the ascendant, grave and stern as himself: another we call 'mercurial,' or light-hearted, as those born under the planet Mercury were accounted to be. The same faith in the influence of the stars survives in 'disastrous,' 'ill-starred,' 'ascendancy,' 'lord of the ascendant,' and, indeed, in 'influence' itself. Again, what curious legends belong to the 'sardonic,' or 'Sardinian'† laugh; a laugh caused, as

---

* 'Jovial' in Shakespeare's time (see *Cymbeline*, Act 5, Sc. 4) had not forgotten its connexion with Jove.

† See an excellent history of this word in Rost and Palm's *Greek Lexicon*, s. v. σαρδάνιος.

was supposed, by a plant in Sardinia, of which they who ate, died laughing; to the 'amethyst,' esteemed, as the word implies, a preventive or antidote of drunkenness; and to other words not a few of which are employed by us still.

A question presents itself here, one which is not merely speculative; for it has before now become a veritable case of conscience with some whether they ought to use words which originally rested on, and so seem still to affirm, some superstition or untruth. This question has practically settled itself; the words will keep their ground: but further, they have a right to do this; for no word need be considered so to root itself in its etymology, and to draw its sap and strength from thence, that it cannot detach itself from this, and acquire the rights of an independent existence. And thus our *weekly* newspapers commit no absurdity in calling themselves '*journals*;' we involve ourselves in no real contradiction, speaking of a 'quarantine' of five, ten, or any number of days more or fewer than *forty*; the wax of our 'candles' ('candela,' from 'candeo') is not necessarily *white*; our 'rubrics' are such still, though seldom printed in *red* ink. I remember once asking a class of school-children, whether an announcement which during one very hard winter appeared in the papers, of a '*white black*bird' having been shot, was correctly worded, or self-contradictory and absurd. The less thoughtful members of the class instantly pronounced against it; while after a little consideration, two or three made answer that it was perfectly correct, that, while no doubt the bird had originally obtained this name from its blackness, yet 'black-bird' was now the name of a species, and one so cleaving to it, as not to be forfeited, even when the blackness had quite disappeared. We do not question the right of the '*New* Forest' to retain this title, though it has now stood for nigh eight hundred years; nor of 'Naples' to be *New* City (Neapolis) still, after an existence three or four times as long.

It must, then, be esteemed a piece of ethical prudery, and an ignorance of the laws which languages obey, when the early Quakers refused to employ the names commonly given to the days of the week, and substituted for these, 'first day,' 'second day,' and so on. This they did, as is well known, on the ground that it became not Christian men to give the sanction to idolatry which was involved in the ordinary style—as though every time they spoke of Wednesday they would be rendering some homage to Woden, of Thursday to Thor, of Friday to Freya, and thus with the rest.*
Now it is quite intelligible that the early Chris-

---

* It is curious to find Fuller prophesying, a very few years before, that at some future day such a protest as theirs might actually be raised (*Church History*, b. ii. cont. 6): 'Thus we see the whole week bescattered with Saxon idols, whose pagan gods were the godfathers of the days, and gave them their names. This some zealot may behold as the object of a necessary reformation, desiring to have the days of the week now dipt, and called after other names. Though, indeed, this supposed scandal will not offend the wise, as beneath their notice; and cannot offend the ignorant, as above their knowledge.'

tians, living in the midst of a still rampant heathenism, should have objected, as we know they did, to 'dies *Solis*,' or Sunday, to express the first day of the week, their Lord's-Day. But when the Quakers raised *their* protest, the case was altogether different. The false gods whose names were bound up in these words had ceased to be worshipped in England for about a thousand years; the words were wholly disengaged from their etymologies, which not one in a hundred was so much as aware of. Moreover, had these precisians in speech been consistent, they would not have stopped where they did. Every new acquaintance with the etymology or primary use of words would have entangled them in new embarrassment, would have required them still further to purge their vocabulary. 'To charm,' 'to bewitch,' 'to fascinate,' 'to enchant,' would have been no longer lawful words for those who had outlived the belief in magic, and in the power of the evil eye; nor 'lunacy,' nor 'lunatic,' for such as did not consider that the moon had anything to do with mental unsoundness; nor 'panic' fear, for those who believed that the great god Pan was indeed dead; nor 'auguries,' nor 'auspices,' for those to whom divination was nothing; while to speak of 'initiating' a person into the 'mysteries' of an art, would have been utterly heathenish language. Nay, they must have found fault with the language of Holy Scripture itself; for a word of honourable use in the New Testament, expressing the function of an interpreter (it re-appears in our 'hermeneutics'), is directly derived from and embodies the name of Hermes, a heathen deity, and one who did not, like Woden, Thor, and Freya, pertain to a long extinct mythology, but to one existing at that very moment in its strength. And how was it, we may ask, that St. Paul did not protest against a Christian woman retaining the name of Phœbe (Rom. xvi. 1), a goddess of the same mythology?

After all which has thus been adduced, you will scarcely deny that we have a right to speak of a history in words. Now suppose that the pieces of money which in the intercourse and traffic of daily life are passing through our hands, had each one something of its own which made it more or less worthy of note; if on one was stamped some striking maxim, on another some important fact, on a third a memorable date; if others were works of finest art, graven with rare and beautiful devices, or bearing the head of some ancient sage or heroic king; while others, again, were the sole surviving monuments of mighty nations that once filled the world with their fame; what a careless indifference to our own improvement—to all which men hitherto had felt or wrought—would it argue in us, if we were content that these should come and go, should stay by us or pass from us, without our vouchsafing to them so much as one serious regard. Such a currency there is, a currency intellectual and spiritual of no meaner worth, and one with which we have to transact so much of the higher business of our lives. Let us see that we come not in this matter under the condemnation of any such incurious dulness as that which I have imagined.

LECTURE V.

ON THE RISE OF NEW WORDS.

YOU will find it not less interesting than instructive to take note of the periods when great and significant words, or sometimes such as can hardly claim these epithets, have risen up, with the circumstances attending their rise. Hardly less interesting than these are new uses of old words. The different portions of my subject so run into one another, that this matter I have, though unwillingly, already anticipated in part; yet it is one which abundantly deserves a lecture to itself. Indeed I am persuaded that a volume might be written, such as would have few to rival it in interest, which should do no more than indicate, and, where advisable, quote the first writer or the first document wherein a new word, or an old word employed in a new sense—being words that have afterwards played an important part in the world's history—has appeared. An English poet, too early lost, has very grandly described the emotion of—

> 'some watcher of the skies,
> When a new planet swims into his ken.'

The feeling wherewith we watch the rise above

the horizon of words, destined it may be to shine for ever as luminaries in the moral and intellectual heaven above us, will not be very different from his.

At the same time a caution is needful here. We must not assume in every case, or indeed in most cases, that the first rise of a word, and its first appearance within the scope of our vision, will be identical. Sometimes they will be so; and we may watch the actual birth of a word, and affirm with confidence that at such a time and on such an occasion it first saw the light—in this book, or from the lips of that man. With respect to another we can only say, About this time and near about this spot it first came into being, for we first meet it in such an author and under such and such conditions. So much of ancient literature has perished, so mere a fragment of it has come down to us, that while the earliest appearance there of a word is still most instructive to note, it can with no confidence be affirmed to mark the time of its first existence. And even in the modern world we must in most instances be contented to fix a period, perhaps also a locality, within the limits of which the term must have been born, either in legitimate scientific travail, or the child of some flash of genius, or the produce of some *generatio aequivoca*, the necessary result of exciting predisposing causes; at the same time seeking by further research ever to narrow this period more and more.

To speak first of words religious and ecclesiastical,—very noteworthy, and in some sort epoch-making, must be regarded the first appearance of these—'Christian;'[1] 'Trinity;'[2] 'Catholic' as applied to the Church;'[3] 'canonical,' as a distinctive title of the received Scriptures;[4] 'New Testament,' as describing the complex of the sacred books of the New Covenant;[5] 'Gospels,' as applied to the four inspired records of the life of our Lord.[6] We notice, too, with interest the first coming up of 'monk' and 'nun,'[7] marking as they do the beginnings of the monastic system;—of 'transubstantiation,'[8] of 'limbo'[9] in its theological sense; witnessing as these do to the *consolidation* of errors which had long been floating in the Church. Very instructive, too, is it to note the earliest apparition of names historical and geographical, above all such as have since been often on the lips of men; as the first mention which we have of 'India;'[10] of 'Europe;'[11] of 'Macedonia;'[12] of 'Germans' and 'Germany;'[13] of 'Alemanni;'[14]

---

[1] Acts xi. 26.
[2] Tertullian, *Adv. Prax.* c. 3.
[3] Ignatius, *Ad Smyr.* c. 8.
[4] Origen, *Opp.* v. 3. p. 36. (ed. de la Rue).
[5] Tertullian, *Adv. Marc.* 4. 1; *Adv. Prax.* 15. 20.
[6] Justin Martyr, *Apol.* 1. 66.
[7] 'Nun' (nonna) first appears in Jerome (*Ad Eustoch.* Ep. 22); 'monk' (monachus) a little earlier: Rutilius, a Latin versifier, who still clung to the old Paganism, gives the derivation:

Ipsi se *monachos* Graio cognomine dicunt,
Quod *soli* nullo vivere teste volunt.

[8] Hildebert, Bishop of Tours, *Serm.* 93. He died in 1134.
[9] Thomas Aquinas is the first to use 'limbus' in this sense.
[10] Æschylus, *Suppl.* 282.   [11] Herodotus, iv. 36.
[12] Herodotus, v. 17.
[13] Probably first in the *Commentaries* of Cæsar.
[14] Spartian, *Caracalla,* c. 9.

of 'Franks;'[1] of 'Prussians'[2] of 'Normans;'[3] the earliest notice by any Greek author of Rome;[4] the first use of 'Italy' as embracing the entire Hesperian peninsula,[5] of 'Asia Minor' to designate the Asia on this side Taurus.[6] Interesting is it to note who it was that first gave to the newly discovered continent in the West the name of 'America,' and when;[7] and to us Englishmen far more interesting the time when this island exchanged its earlier name of Britain for 'Anglia' or 'England;' or, again, when it resumed 'Great Britain' as its official designation. So also, to confirm our assertion by examples from another quarter, it cannot be unprofitable to mark the exact moment at which 'tyrant' and 'tyranny,' forming so distinct an epoch as it does in the political history of Greece, first appeared;[8] when,

---

[1] Vopiscus, *Aurel.* c. 7; about A.D. 240.
[2] 'Pruzzi' and 'Pruzia' first appear in the *Life of St. Adalbert*, written by his fellow-labourer Gaudentius, between 997-1006.
[3] In the *Geographer of Ravenna.*
[4] Probably in Hellanicus, a cotemporary of Herodotus.
[5] In the time of Augustus Cæsar.
[6] Orosius, 1. 2: in the fifth century of our era.
[7] See p. 123.
[8] In the writings of Archilochus, about 700 B.C. A 'tyrant' was not for Greeks a bad king, who abused a rightful position to purposes of lust or cruelty or other wrong. It was of the essence of such that he had attained supreme dominion through a violation of the laws and liberties of the state; having done which, whatever the moderation of his after-rule, he would not escape the name. Thus the mild and bounteous Pisistratus was 'tyrant' of Athens, while a Christian the Second of Denmark, 'the Nero of the North,' would not in Greek eyes have been one. It was to their honour that they did not allow the course of the word to be arrested or turned aside by occasional or partial exceptions in the manner of the exorcise of this ill-gotten dominion; but in the

and from whom, the fabric of the external universe first received the title of 'cosmos,' or beautiful order;* with much more of the same kind.

Take, for instance, 'Christian.' We have here the Holy Spirit Himself counting a name and the coming up of a name so important as to cause that it should find special record in the Book of life: 'The disciples were called Christians first in Antioch' (Acts xi. 26). That it is a notice curious and interesting, all would acknowledge, as everything must be which relates to the infancy of the Church. Some, perhaps, would see in it nothing more; and yet, if we question this notice a little closer, how much it contains, and is waiting to yield up to us. What light it throws on the whole story of the apostolic Church to know where and when this name of 'Christians' was first imposed on the faithful; for imposed by adversaries it certainly was, not devised by themselves, however afterwards they may have learned to glory in it as the name of highest dignity and honour. They did not call themselves, but as is expressly recorded, they 'were called' Christians first at Antioch; in agreement with which statement, the name occurs no where in Scripture, except on the lips of those alien

---

hateful secondary sense which 'tyrant' with them acquired, and which we have adopted, the moral conviction, justified by all experience, spake out, that the ill-gotten would be ill-kept; that the 'tyrant' in the earlier sense of the word, dogged by suspicion, fear, and an evil conscience, must, by an almost inevitable law, become a 'tyrant' in our later sense of the word.

* The word is ascribed to Pythagoras, born B.C. 570.

from, or opposed to, the faith (Acts xxvi. 28; 1 Pet. iv. 16). And as it was a name imposed by adversaries, so among those adversaries it was plainly the heathen, and not the Jews, who were its authors; for these last would never have called the followers of Jesus of Nazareth, 'Christians,' or those of Christ, the very point of their opposition to Him being, that He was *not* the Christ, but a false pretender to the name.*

Starting then from this point, that 'Christians' was a title given to the disciples by the heathen, what may we learn from it more? At Antioch they first obtained this name—at the city, that is, which was the head-quarters of the Church's missions to the heathen, in the same sense as Jerusalem had been the head-quarters of those to the seed of Abraham. It was there, and among the faithful there, that a conviction of the world-wide destination of the Gospel arose; there it was first plainly seen as intended for all kindreds of the earth. Hitherto the faithful in Christ had been called by their adversaries, and indeed often were still called, 'Galileans,' or 'Nazarenes,'—both names which indicated the Jewish cradle in which the Church had been nursed, and that the world saw in the new society no more than a Jewish sect. But it was plain that the Church had now,

---

* Comparo Tacitus (*Annal.* xv. 24): Quos *vulgus* . . . Christianos appellabat. It is curious too that, although a Greek word and coined in a Greek city, the termination is Latin. Χριστιανός is formed on the model of Romanus, Albanus, Pompeianus, and the like.

even in the world's eyes, chipped its Jewish shell. The name 'Christians,' or those of Christ, while it told that Christ and the confession of Him was felt even by the heathen to be the sum and centre of this new faith, showed also that they comprehended now, not all which the Church would be, but what it claimed to be,—no mere variation of Judaism, but a Society with a mission and destination of its own. Nor will the thoughtful reader fail to observe that the coming up of this name is by closest juxtaposition connected in the sacred narrative, and still more closely in the Greek than in the English, with the arrival at Antioch and the preaching there of that Apostle, who was God's appointed instrument for bringing the Church into the recognition of its destination for all men. As so often happens with the rise of new names, the rise of this one marked a new epoch in the Church's life, and that it was entering upon a new stage of its development. It is a small matter, yet not without its own interest, that the invention of this name is laid by St. Luke,—for so, I think, we may confidently say,—to the credit of the Antiochenes. Now the idle, frivolous, and witty inhabitants of Antioch were famous in all antiquity for the invention of nicknames; it was a manufacture for which their city was famous. And thus it was exactly the place, where beforehand we might have expected that such a title, being a nickname or little better in their mouths who devised it, should first come into being.

Our other example shall be 'Anglia,' or 'England.' When and under what circumstances did this island exchange for this the earlier name of Britain, which it had borne for more than a thousand years? There seems no sufficient reason for calling in question, though some have so done, the statement of the old chronicler that it received this new name of 'Anglia' from Egbert, king of Wessex, who with the sanction of his Witanegemot, held A.D. 800 in this very city of Winchester, determined that the name 'Britain' should give place to 'England.' It may be that the change was not effected by any such formal act as this, yet the accuracy of the old annalist, so far at least as his date is concerned, receives confirmation from the circumstance that 'Anglia,' nowhere to be traced in documents anterior to this period, does immediately after begin to appear.

What lessons for the student of English history are here, in the knowledge of this one fact, if he will but seek to look at it all round, and consider it in a thoughtful spirit. I have said that the appearance of a new name marks often a new epoch in history; certainly it was so in the instance before us. In the first place, as it is the just law of names, that a people should give a name to the land which they possess, not receive one from it, as the Franks make Gaul to be France, do not suffer themselves to become Gauls, so, as regards our own land, it is plain from the coming up of this name that there must have been now a sense in men's minds that its transformation from a land of Britons to a land of

Angles was at length completely accomplished, and might therefore justly claim to find its recognition in a word. That the Normans never made a 'Norman-land' out of England, as they had out of Neustria, and as the Angles had made an 'Angle-land' out of Britain,—that they never so supplanted the population, or dissolved the social framework, of the Angles, as these had done of the Britons,—is evident from the fact that there went along with *their* conquest of the land no such substitution of a new name for the old, no such obliteration of the old by the new, as on that prior occupation of the soil had found place.

And then further, how significant a fact, that the invading German tribes, which had hitherto been content to call themselves according to the different provinces or districts which they occupied, should have now felt that they needed, and out of that need should have given birth to, a name common to and including the whole land. Was there not here a sign that the sense of unity, of all making up one corporate body, one nation, was emerging out of the confusion of the preceding period of the Heptarchy? We know from other sources that Egbert was the first who united the different kingdoms of the Heptarchy under his single sceptre; the first in whom the nation was knit together into one. How instructive to find a name which should be the symbol of unity, coming to the birth at this very moment. In respect too of the relations between themselves of the two most important tribes which had settled

V. THE CAUSES OF NEW WORDS. 145

in this island, the Angles and the Saxons (the Jutes were too few to contend for the honour), it is assuredly a weighty fact that it was the Angles alone, from whom, though numerically inferior, the new appellation was derived. Doubtless, a moral or political predominance of this tribe, probably a political founded on a moral, asserted itself in this fact. We are the less inclined to attribute it to accident from the circumstance that in the phrase 'Anglo-Saxons' (Angli-Saxones), which is no modern invention of convenience, as is sometimes erroneously asserted, but is of earlier use even than Anglia, the Angles have again the precedence, and the Saxons only follow.

These examples show that new words will often repay any attention which we may bestow upon them, and upon the conditions under which they were born. I proceed to consider the causes of their birth, the periods when a language is most fruitful in them, the quarters from which they usually proceed, with some other interesting phenomena about them.

And first of the causes which give them birth. The cause which more than any other makes new words necessary, and evokes the words which shall supply this necessity, is this—namely, that in the appointments of highest Wisdom there are epochs in the world's history, in which, more than at other times, new moral and spiritual forces are at work, stirring to their central depths the hearts of men. When it is thus with a people, they make claims on their language, never made on it before. It is required to utter truths, to express ideas, which were remote from it hitherto; for which therefore the adequate expression will naturally not be forthcoming at once, these new thoughts and feelings being larger and deeper than any with which hitherto the speakers of that tongue had been familiar. It fares with a language then, as it would fare with a river bed, suddenly required to deliver a far larger volume of waters than had hitherto been its wont. It would in such a case be nothing strange, if the waters surmounted their banks, broke forth on the right hand and on the left, forced new channels with something of violence for themselves. This indeed they must do. Now it was exactly thus that it fared—for there could be no more illustrious examples—with the languages of Greece and Rome, when it was demanded of them that they should be vehicles of the truths of revelation.

These languages, as they already existed, might have sufficed, and did suffice, for heathenism, sensuous, and finite; but they did not suffice for the spiritual and infinite, for the truths at once so mighty and so new which claimed to find utterance in the language of men. And thus it continually befel, that the new thought must weave a new garment for itself, those which it found ready made being narrower than that it could wrap itself in them; the new wine must find new vessels for itself, that both might be preserved, the old being neither strong enough nor expansive enough to hold it. Thus, not to speak of mere technical matters which would claim an utterance, how could the Greek language possess a word for 'idolatry,' so long as the sense of the awful contrast between the worship of the living God and of dead things had not risen up in their minds that spoke it? But when Greek began to be the native language of men, to whom this distinction and contrast was the most earnest and deepest conviction of their lives, words such as 'idolatry,' 'idolater,' of necessity appeared. The heathen did not claim for their deities to be 'searchers of hearts,' did not disclaim for them the being 'accepters of persons;' such attributes of power and righteousness entered not into their minds as pertaining to the objects of their worship. The Greek language, therefore, so long as they only employed it, had not the words corresponding. It, indeed, could not have had them, as the Jewish Hellenistic Greek could not be without them. Where, in like manner, except in the bosom of the same Jewish Greek could the word 'theocracy' have been born?*

These difficulties, which would be felt the most strongly when the thought and feeling that had been at home in the Hebrew, the original language of inspiration, needed to be transferred into Greek, reappeared, though not in quite so aggravated a form, when that which had gradually woven for itself in the Greek an adequate array, again

---

* We preside at its birth in a passage of Josephus, *Con. Apion.* ii. 16.

demanded to find a suitable attire in the Latin. A single example of the difficulty, and of the way in which it was ultimately overcome, will illustrate this far better than long disquisitions. The Greek had a word for 'saviour,' which, though often degraded to unworthy uses, bestowed as a title of honour not merely on the false gods of heathendom, but sometimes on men, such as better deserved to be styled 'destroyers' than 'saviours' of their fellows, was yet in itself not unequal to the setting forth the central office and dignity of Him, who came into the world to save it. It was a word which might be likened to some profaned temple, not needing to be abolished and another built in its room, but only to be consecrated anew. With the Latin it was otherwise. The language seemed to be without a word, which in one shape or another Christians needed to have continually on their lips: indeed Cicero, than whom none could know better the resources of his own tongue, remarkably enough had noted that it possessed no single word corresponding to the Greek 'saviour.'*
'Salvator' would have been the natural word; but literary Latin, though it had 'salus' and 'salvus,' had neither this, nor the verb 'salvare;' some, indeed, have thought that 'salvare' had always existed in the common speech. 'Servator' was instinctively felt to be insufficient, even as 'Preserver' would for us fall very short of utter-

---

* Hoc [σωτήρ] quantum est? ita magnum ut Latinè uno verbo exprimi non possit.

ing all which 'Saviour' does now. The seeking of the strayed, the recovering of the lost, the healing of the sick, would all be feebly and faintly insinuated by it. God '*preserveth* man and beast,' but He is the 'Saviour' of his own in a more inward and far tenderer sense. It was long before the Latin Christian writers extricated themselves from this embarrassment, for the 'Salutificator' of Tertullian, the 'Sospitator' of another, did not assuredly satisfy the need. The strong good sense of Augustine finally disposed of the difficulty. He made no scruple about using 'Salvator;' observing well, and with a true insight into the law of the birth of words, that however 'Salvator' might not have been good Latin before the Saviour came, He by his coming made it such; for, as shadows wait upon substances, so words follow upon things.*

But it is not only when new truth, coming directly from God, has thus to fit itself to the lips of men, that such enlargements of speech become necessary: but in each further unfolding

---

* *Serm.* 299. 6: Christus Jesus, id est Christus Salvator: hoc est enim Latinè Jesus. Nec quærant grammatici quàm sit Latinum, sed Christiani, quàm verum. Salus enim Latinum nomen est; salvare et salvator non fuerunt hæc Latina, antequam veniret Salvator: quando ad Latinos venit, et hæc Latina fecit. Cf. *De Trin.* 13. 10: Quod verbum [salvator] Latina lingua antea non habebat, sed habere poterat; sicut potuit quando voluit. Other words which we owe to Christian Latin, not to speak of such purely technical as 'incarnatio,' are 'deitas' (Augustine, *Civ. Dei*, 7. 1), 'resipiscentia,' 'passio,' 'compassio,' 'longanimitas,' 'tribulatio,' 'soliloquium,' 'carnalis.'

of those seminal truths implanted in man at the first, in each new enlargement of his sphere of knowledge, outward or inward, lie the same necessities involved. The beginnings and progressive advances of moral philosophy in Greece, the transplanting of the same to Rome, the rise of the scholastic, and then of the mystic, theology in the middle ages, the discoveries of modern science and natural philosophy, all these have been accompanied with corresponding extensions in the limits of language. Of the words to which each of these has in turn given birth many, it is true, have never passed beyond their own peculiar sphere, having remained technical, scientific, or purely theological to the last; but many, too, have passed over from the laboratory, the school, and the pulpit, into daily life, and have, with the ideas which they incorporate, become the common heritage of all. For however hard and repulsive a front any study or science may seem to present to the great body of those who are as laymen to it, there is yet inevitably such a detrition as this going forward in the case of each, and it would not be a little interesting for one who was furnished with the knowledge sufficient, to trace it in all.

Where the movement is a popular one, stirring the heart and mind of a people to its very depths, there these new words will be for the most part born out of their bosom, a free spontaneous birth, seldom or never capable of being referred to one man more than another, because they belong to all. Where, on the contrary, the movement is more strictly theological, or has for its sphere those regions of science and philosophy, where, as first pioneers and discoverers, only a few can bear their parts, there the additions and extensions will lack something of the freedom, the unconscious boldness, which mark the others. Their character will be more artificial, less spontaneous, although here also the creative genius of the single man, as there of the nation, will oftentimes set its mark; and many a single word will come forth, which will be the result of profound meditation, or of intuitive genius, or of both in happiest combination—many a word, which shall as a torch illuminate vast regions comparatively obscure before, and, it may be, cast its rays far into the yet unexplored darkness beyond; or which, summing up into itself all the acquisitions in a particular direction of the past, shall be as a mighty vantage ground from which to advance to new conquests in those realms of mind or of nature, not as yet subdued to the intellect of man.

'Cosmopolite' has often now a shallow or even a mischievous use, and he who calls himself such may mean nothing more than that he is *not* a patriot, that his native country does *not* possess his love. Yet he could not have been a common man who, before the preaching of the Gospel, composed this word. Nor was he; for Diogenes the Cynic, whose sayings are among the most notable in antiquity, was its author. Being demanded of what city or country he was, Diogenes answered that he was a 'cosmopolite;' in this word, which he thus launched upon the world, widening the range of men's thoughts, bringing in not merely a word new to Greek ears, but a thought which, however commonplace to us, was most novel and startling to those whom he addressed. I am far from saying that contempt for his citizenship in its narrower sense may not have mingled with this his challenge for himself of a citizenship wide as the world; but there was not the less a very remarkable reaching out here after truths which were not fully borne into the world until the Son of God came.

As occupying something of a middle place between those more deliberate word-makers, and the people whose words rather grow than are made, we must not omit him who is a *maker* by the very right of his name—I mean, the poet. That creative energy with which he is endowed, 'the high-flying liberty of conceit proper to the poet,' will in all probability manifest itself in this region as in others. Extending the domain of thought and feeling, he will scarcely fail to extend that also of language, which does not willingly lag behind. And the loftier his moods, the more of this maker he will be. The passion of such times, the all-fusing imagination, will at once suggest and justify audacities in speech, upon which in calmer moods he would not venture, or, if he ventured, would fail to carry others with him: for only the fluent metal runs easily into novel shapes and moulds. It is not merely that the old and the familiar will often become new in his hands; that he will give the stamp of allowance, as to him it will be free to do, to words, should he count them worthy, which hitherto have lived only on the lips of the multitude, or been confined to some single dialect and province; but he will enrich his native tongue with words unknown and non-existent before— non-existent, that is, save in their elements; for in the historic period of a language it is not permitted to any man to bring new roots into it, but only to work on already given materials; to evolve what is latent therein, to combine what is apart, to recall what has fallen out of sight.

But to return to the more deliberate coining of words. New necessities have within the last few years called out several of these deliberate creations in our own language. The discovery of such large abundance of gold in so many quarters of the world has led some nations so much to dread an enormous fall in its value, that they have ceased to make it the standard of value—Holland, for instance, has so done—and it has been found convenient to invent a word, 'to demonetize,' to express this process of turning a precious metal from being the legal standard into a mere article of commerce. So, too, diplomacy has added more than one new word to our vocabulary during the last twenty years. I suppose nobody ever heard of 'extradition' till then; nor of 'neutralization' till in the peace which followed the Crimean War, the 'neutralization' of the Black Sea was one of the stipulations. Our manifold contact with the East, with the necessity which has thence arisen of representing Oriental words by aid of altogether a different alphabet, and the discussion how this best may be done, has brought with it the need of possessing a word to describe the process, and 'transliteration' is the result.

But it is not merely new things which will require new names. It will often be discovered that old things have not got one. The manner in which men most often become aware of such deficiencies, is through the comparison of their own language with another, and, in some provinces at least, a richer. Such comparison is forced upon them, so that they cannot put it by, as soon as it has become necessary for them to express in their own tongue that which has already found utterance in another, and has thus shown that it is utterable in human speech. Without such a comparison the absence of the needful terms would probably seldom dawn even on the most thoughtful; for language is to so great an extent the condition and limit of thought, men are so little accustomed, indeed so little able, to meditate on things, except through the intervention, and by the machinery, of words, that nothing short of this would bring them to a sense of the actual existence of any such wants. It is, I may observe, one of the advantages of acquaintance with another language besides our own, and of the institution which will follow, if we have learned that other to any purpose, of these comparisons, that we thus become aware that names are not, and least of all the names which any single language possesses, co-extensive with things (and by 'things' I mean subjects as well as objects of thought, whatever one can *think* about), that a multitude of things exist which, though capable of being resumed and connoted in a word, are yet without one, unnamed and unregistered; so that, vast as is the world of names, the world of realities is even vaster still. Such discoveries the Romans made, when they attempted to transplant the moral philosophy of Greece to an Italian soil. They found that many of its terms had no equivalents in their own tongue; which equivalents therefore they proceeded with more or less success to devise for themselves, appealing for this to the latent capabilities of their own tongue. For example, the Greek schools had a word, and one playing no unimportant part in some of their philosophical systems, to express 'apathy,' or the absence of all passion and pain. As it was absolutely necessary to possess a corresponding word, Cicero invented 'indolentia,' as that 'if I may so speak' with which he paves the way to his first introduction of it, manifestly declares.*

Sometimes, indeed, such a skilful mint-master of words, such a subtle watcher and weigher of their force† as was Cicero, will note, even apart from this comparison with other languages, an omission in his own, which thereupon he will endeavour to supply. Thus the Latin had two

---

* *Fin.* 2. 4; and for 'qualitas' see *Acad.* 1. 6.
† Ille verborum vigilantissimus appensor ac mensor, as Augustine happily terms him.

adjectives which, though sometimes confusedly used, possessed each its peculiar meaning, 'invidus,' one who is envious, 'invidiosus,' one who excites envy in others;* at the same time there was only one substantive, 'invidia,' the correlative of them both; with the disadvantage, therefore, of being employed now in an active, now in a passive sense, now for the envy which men feel, and now for the envy which they excite. The word he saw was made to do double duty, and that under a seeming unity there lurked a real dualism, from which manifold confusions might follow. He therefore devised 'invidentia,' to express the active envy, or the envying, no doubt desiring that 'invidia' should be restrained to the passive, the being envied. 'Invidentia' to all appearance supplied a real want; yet he did not succeed in giving it currency; does not seem himself to have much cared to employ it again.†

We see by this example that not every word, which even a master of language proposes, finds acceptance.‡ Provided some live, he must be contented that others should fall to the ground and die. Nor is this the only unsuccessful candidate for admission into the language which Cicero proposed. His 'indolentia,' which I mentioned

---

* Thus the monkish line:
    Invidiosus ego, non *invidus* esse laboro.

† *Tusc.* 3. 9; 4. 8; cf. Döderlein, *Synon.* vol. iii. p. 68.

‡ Quintilian's advice, based on this fact, is good (1. 6, 42): Etiamsi potest nihil peccare, qui utitur iis verbis quæ summi auctores tradiderunt, multum tamen refert non solùm quid *dixerint,* sed etiam quid *persuaserint.*

just now, hardly passed beyond himself;* his 'vitiositas,'† 'indigentia,' and ' mulierositas,'‡ not at all. 'Beatitas' too and 'beatitudo,'§ both of his coining, yet, as he owns himself, with something strange and uncouth about them, found but the faintest echo in the classical literature of Rome: 'beatitudo,' indeed, obtained a home, as it deserved to do, in the Christian Church, but 'beatitas' made no way whatsoever. Coleridge's 'esemplastic,' which pleased himself so much, has obtained no favour with others; while the words of Jeremy Taylor, of such Latinists as Sir Thomas Browne and Henry More, words born only to die, are multitudinous as the leaves of autumn. Still even the word which fails is often an honourable testimony to the scholarship, the accuracy of thought, the imagination of its proposer; and Ben Jonson is overhard on 'neologists,' if I may bring this term back to its earlier meaning, when he says: 'A man coins not a new word without some peril, and less fruit; for if it happen to be received, the praise is but moderate; if refused, the scorn is assured.'

I spoke just now of comprehensive words, which should singly say what hitherto it had taken many words to say, in which a higher term has been reached than before had been found. The

---

* Thus Seneca a little later has forgotten, or is unaware, that Cicero made any such suggestion. Taking no notice of it, he proposes 'impatientia' as an adequate rendering of ἀνδρεία, which indeed had the inconvenience, as he himself allows, that it was already used in exactly the opposite sense (*Ep.* 9).

† *Tusc.* 4. 15. ‡ *Tusc.* 4. 11. § *Nat. Deor.* 1. 34.

value of these is immense. By the cutting short
of lengthy explanations and tedious circuits of
language, they facilitate mental processes, which
would often be nearly or quite impossible without
them; and those who have invented or put these
into circulation, are benefactors of a high order to
knowledge. In the ordinary traffic of life, unless
our dealings were on the smallest scale, we should
willingly have about us our money in the shape
rather of silver than of copper; and if our transactions were at all extensive, rather in gold than
in silver; while, if we were setting forth upon a
long and costly journey, we should be best pleased
to turn even our gold coin itself into bills of exchange or circular notes; in fact, into the highest
denomination of money which it was capable of
assuming. How many words with which we are
now perfectly familiar are for us what bills of exchange or circular notes are for the traveller and
the merchant. As in one of these last, innumerable pence, a multitude of shillings, not a few
pounds are gathered up and represented, so
have we in some single word the quintessence
and final result of an infinite number of anterior mental processes, ascending one above
the other, until all have been at length summed
up for us in that single word. This is like to
nothing so much as to some mighty river, which
does not bring its flood of waters to the sea, till
many rills have been swallowed up in brooks,
and brooks in streams, and streams in tributary
rivers, each of these affluents having lost its

separate name and existence in that which at once at last represents and is continent of them all.

Science is often an immense gainer by words which thus say singly, what whole sentences would otherwise have scarcely said. Thus 'isothermal' is quite a modern invention; but how much is summed up by the word; what a long story is saved, as often as we speak of 'isothermal' lines. Take even a word so familiar as 'circle.' How much must have gone before, ere the word, with its corresponding idea, could have existed; and then imagine how it would fare with us, if, as often as in some long and difficult mathematical problem we needed to refer to this figure, we were obliged to introduce its entire definition, no single word representing it; and not this only, but the definition of each term employed in the definition;—how well nigh impossible it would prove to carry the whole process in the mind, or to take oversight of all its steps. Imagine a few more words struck out of the vocabulary of the mathematician, and if all mental activity in his proper domain was not altogether arrested, yet would it be as effectually restrained and hampered as commercial intercourse would be, if in all its transactions iron or copper were the sole medium of exchange. Wherever any science is progressive, there will be progress in its nomenclature as well. Words will keep pace with things, and with more or less felicity resuming in themselves the labours of the past, will at once assist and abridge the labours of the future; like tools which, themselves the result of the finest mechanical skill, do at the same time render other and further triumphs of art possible, such as would have been quite unattainable without them.

It is not merely the widening of men's intellectual horizon, which, bringing new thoughts within the range of their vision, compels the origination of corresponding words; but as often as regions of this outward world hitherto closed are laid open, the novel objects of interest which these contain will demand to find their names, and not merely to be catalogued in the nomenclature of science, but, so far as they present themselves to the popular eye, will require to be popularly named. When a new thing, a plant, or fruit, or animal, or whatever else it may be, is imported from some foreign land, or so comes within the sphere of knowledge that it needs to be thus named, there are various ways in which this may be done. The first and commonest way is to import the name and the thing together, incorporating the former, unchanged, or with slight modification, into the language. Thus we did with the potatoe, which is only another form of 'batata,' in which shape the original Indian word appears in our earlier voyagers. But this is not the only way of naming; and the example on which I have just lighted affords good illustration of various other methods which may be adopted. Thus a name belonging to something else, which the new object nearly resembles, may be transferred to it, and the confusion arising from calling different things by the same name disregarded. It was thus in German, 'Kartoffel' being only a corruption, which found place in the last century, of 'Tartuffel,' properly the name of the truffle; but which not the less was transferred to the potatoe, on the ground of the many resemblances between them. Or again this same transfer may take place, but with some qualifying or distinguishing addition. This course the Italians took. They also called the potatoe 'tartufo,' but added 'bianco,' the white truffle;—the name is now giving way to 'patata.' Thus was it, too, with the French; who called it apple, but 'apple of the earth' (pomme de terre); even as in many of the provincial dialects of Germany it bears the name of 'Erdappel' or earth-apple at this day.

It will sometimes happen that a language, having thus to provide a new name for a new thing, will for a time seem not to have made up its mind by which of those methods it shall do it. Two names will exist side by side, and only after a time will one gain the upper hand of the other. Thus when the pineapple was introduced into England it brought with it, probably from the East, the name 'ananas' or 'anana,' under which last form it is celebrated by Thomson in his *Seasons*. This name has been nearly or quite put out of use by 'pineapple,' manifestly derived from the likeness of the new fruit to the cone of the pine. It is not a very happy formation; for it is not *likeness* but *identity* which the word implies; and it gives some excuse to an error, which up to a very late day ran through all German-English and French-English dictionaries (I know not whether it is even now removed); in all of these 'pineapple' is rendered as though it signified not the anana, but this cone of the pine; and not very long ago, the foremost newspaper in France made some uncomplimentary observations on the voracity of the English, who could wind up a Lord Mayor's dinner with fir-cones for dessert.

Sometimes the name adopted will be one drawn from an intermediate language, through which the knowledge first reached us of the object requiring to be named. 'Alligator' is an example of this; an example, too, of the manner in which, at some periods in the life of a language, everything turns to good, so that mistakes and errors, misshaping, and seeming to mar a word at its first formation, yet do not hinder it from forming a serviceable portion of the after tongue. When the alligator, that ugly crocodile of the New World, was first seen by the Spanish discoverers, they called it, with a true insight into its species, 'el lagarto,' or *the* lizard, as being the largest of that lizard species to which it belonged, or indeed sometimes 'el lagarto de las Indias,' the Indian lizard. In Sir Walter Raleigh's *Discovery of Guiana*, the word still retains its Spanish form. Sailing up the Orinoco, 'We saw in it,' he says, 'divers sorts of strange fishes of marvellous bigness, but for *lagartos* it exceeded; for there were thousands of these ugly serpents, and the people call it, for the abundance of them, the river of *lagartos*, in their language.' We can explain the shape which with us it gradually assumed, by supposing that English sailors who brought it home, and had continually heard, but may have never seen it written, blended, as in similar instances has often happened, the Spanish article 'el' with the name. In Ben Jonson's 'alligarta,' we see the word in the process of transformation.*

Less honourable causes than some which I have mentioned, give birth to new words; which will sometimes reflect back a very fearful light on the moral condition of that epoch in which first they saw the light. Of the Roman emperor, Tiberius, one of those 'inventors of evil things,' of whom St. Paul speaks (Rom. i. 30), Tacitus informs us that he caused words, unknown before, to emerge in the Latin tongue, for the setting out of wicked-

---

* 'Alcoran' supplies another example of this curious annexation of the article. Examples of a like absorption or incorporation of it are numerous in French. 'Lierre,' ivy, was written by Ronsard, 'l'hierre,' which is correct, being the Latin 'hedera.' 'Lingot' is our 'ingot,' but with fusion of the article. In old French it was 'l'endemain,' or, le jour en demain : 'le lendemain,' as now written, is a barbarous excess of expression. 'La Pouille,' a name given to the southern extremity of Italy, and in which we recognize 'Apulia,' is another variety of error, but moving in the same sphere (Génin, *Récréations Philologiques*, vol. i. pp. 102–105). An Irish scholar has observed that in modern Irish 'an' (= 'the') is frequently thus absorbed in the names of places, as in 'Nenagh,' 'Naul ;' while sometimes an error exactly the reverse of this is committed, and a letter, supposed to be the article, but in fact a part of the word, dropt ; thus 'Oughaval,' instead of 'Noughaval,' or New Habitation.

nesses, happily also previously unknown, which he had invented.

The atrocious attempt of Louis the Fourteenth to convert to Romanism the Protestants in his dominions by quartering dragoons upon them, with license to misuse to the uttermost those who refused to apostatize, this 'booted mission' (mission bottée), as it was facetiously called at the time, has bequeathed 'dragonnade' to the French language. 'Refugee' had at the same time its rise, and owed it to the same event. They were called 'refugiés' or 'refugees' who took refuge in some land less inhospitable than their own, so to escape the tender mercies of these missionaries. 'Convertisseur' belongs to the same period. The factor was so named who undertook to convert the Protestants on a large scale, and at so much a head.

Our use of 'roué' throws light upon a curious and shameful page of history. The 'roué,' a man now of profligate character and conduct, was properly and primarily one broken on the wheel. Its present and secondary meaning it derived from that Duke of Orleans who was Regent of France after the death of Louis the Fourteenth. It was his miserable pride to gather round him companions if possible worse and wickeder than himself. These he called boastfully his 'roués;' every one of them abundantly deserving to be broken on the wheel,—which was the punishment then reserved in France for the worst malefactors.*

---

* The 'roués' themselves declared that the word expressed rather their readiness to give any proof of their affection, even

When we have learned the pedigree of the word, the man and the age rise up before us, glorying in their shame, and not caring to pay to virtue even that hypocritical homage which vice finds it sometimes convenient to render.

The French Revolution has made, as was to be expected, characteristic contributions to the French language. It gives us some insight into its ugliest side to know that, among other words, it produced the following; 'sansculotte,' 'incivisme,' 'terrorisme,' 'noyade,' 'guillotine,' 'lanterner.' Still later, the French conquests in North Africa, and the pitiless severities with which every attempt at resistance on the part of the free tribes of the interior has been put down and punished, have left their mark upon the language. 'Razzia' has been added to it, and expresses the swift and sudden sweeping away of a tribe, its herds, its crops, and all that belongs to it.

But it would ill become us to look only abroad for examples, when perhaps an equal abundance might be found much nearer home. Words of our own keep record of passages in our history in which we have little reason to glory. Thus 'mob' and 'sham' had their birth in that most disgraceful period of English history, the interval between the Restoration and Revolution. 'I may note,' says one writing toward the end of the reign of Charles the Second, 'that the rabble first changed

---

to the being broken upon the wheel, to their protector and friend.

their title, and were called the "mob" in the assemblies of this [The Green Ribbon] Club. It was their beast of burden, and called first "mobile vulgus," but fell naturally into the contraction of one syllable, and ever since is become proper English.'* Yet much later a writer in *The Spectator* speaks of 'mob' as still only struggling into existence. 'I dare not answer,' he says, 'that mob, rap. pos, incog., and the like will not in time be looked at as part of our tongue.' In regard of 'mob,' the 'mobile' multitude swayed hither and thither by each gust of passion or caprice, this, which *The Spectator* hardly expected, while he confessed it possible, has actually taken place. 'It is one of the many words formally slang, which are now used by our best writers, and received, like pardoned outlaws, into the body of respectable citizens.' Again, though the murdering of poor helpless lodgers, afterwards to sell their bodies for dissection, can only be regarded as the monstrous wickedness of one or two, yet the verb 'to burke,' drawn from the name of a wretch who long pursued this hideous traffic, will be evidence to all after times, unless indeed its origin should be forgotten, to how strange a crime this age of a boasted civilization could give birth.

We must not count as new words properly so called, although they may delay us for a minute, those comic words, most often comic combinations formed at will, in which, as plays and displays of

---

* North, *Examen*, p. 574; for the origin of 'sham' see p. 231.

power, writers ancient and modern have delighted. These for the most part are meant to do service for the moment, and then to pass away. The inventors of them themselves had no intention of fastening them permanently on the language. Thus, among other words Aristophanes coined μελλονικίαω, to loiter like Nicias, with allusion to the delays with which this prudent commander sought to put off the disastrous Sicilian expedition, with not a few other familiar to every scholar. The humour will sometimes consist in their enormous length,* sometimes in their mingled observance and transgression of the laws of the language, as in the 'oculissimus' of Plautus, a comic superlative of oculus; 'occisissimus' of occisus; 'dominissimus' of dominus; as in the 'dosones,' 'dabones,' which in Greek and in medieval Latin were names given to those who were ever promising, ever saying 'I will give,' but never following up promise with performance. Plautus, with his exuberant wit, and exulting in his mastery of the Latin language, is rich in these, 'fustitudinus,' 'ferricreprinus' and the like ; will put together four or five lines consisting wholly of comic combinations thrown off for the occasion.† Of the same character is Butler's 'cynarctomachy,' or battle of a dog and bear. Nor do I suppose that Fuller, when he used 'to avunculize,' to follow in the steps of one's uncle, or Cowper, when

---

* As in the ἀμφιπτολεμοπηδησίστρατος of Eupolis ; the σπερματογοραιολεκιθολαχανοπωλις of Aristophanes.

† *Pers.* iv. 6, 20-23.

he suggested 'extraforaneous' for out of doors, at all proposed them as lasting additions to the language.

Such are some of the sources of increase in the wealth of a language; some of the quarters from which its vocabulary is augmented. There have been, from time to time, those who have so little understood what a language is, and what are the laws which it obeys, that they have sought by decrees of theirs to arrest its growth, pronouncing it to have attained to the limits of its growth, so that it should not henceforward presume to develop itself further. But a language has a life, just as really as a man or as a tree. As a man, it must grow to its full stature; even as it is also submitted to his conditions of decay; as a forest tree, it will defy any feeble bands which should attempt to control its expansion, so long as the principle of growth is in it; as a tree too it will continually, while it casts off some leaves, be putting forth others. And thus all these attempts have utterly failed, even when made under conditions the most favourable for success. The French Academy, containing all or nearly all the most distinguished literary men of France, once sought to exercise such a domination over their own language, and, if any could have succeeded, they might have hoped to do so. But the language recked of their decrees as little as the advancing ocean did of those of Canute. Could they hope to keep out of men's speech, or even out of their books, however they kept out of their own *Dictionary*, such words as 'blague,' 'blagueur,' 'blaguer' because, being born of the people, they had something of the people's mark upon them? After fruitless resistance for a time, they have in cases innumerable been compelled to give way—though in favour of the words just cited they have not done so—yet and in each successive edition of their *Dictionary* to throw open its doors to words which had established themselves in the language, and would hold their ground there, altogether indifferent whether they received the Academy's seal of allowance or not.

Littré has shown a far juster appreciation of the actual facts of language. If ever there was a word born in the streets, and bearing about it the tokens of its birthplace, it is 'gamin;' moreover it cannot be traced farther back than the year 1835; then first it appeared in a book, though it may have lived some while before on the lips of the people; but already it has found a place in the pages of his Dictionary. So has 'flaneur,' so no doubt will 'rococo,' and many more, having the same marks on them as these have. And rightly; for however fashions may descend from the upper classes to the lower, words, such words I mean as constitute the most real additions to the stock of a language, ascend from the lower to the higher, and however the fastidious may oppose or ignore them for awhile, will make a place for themselves there, from which they will not be driven out by the efforts of all the scholars and academicians in the world.

Those who make attempts of this kind strangely forget the means by which that vocabulary of the language with which they are so entirely satisfied that they resent every endeavour to enlarge it, had itself been gotten together,—namely by that very process which they are now seeking by an arbitrary decree to arrest. We so take for granted that words with which we have been always familiar, whose right to form a part of the language no one dreams now of challenging or disputing, have always formed part of it, that we should, I believe, be oftentimes surprised to discover of how very late introduction some of these actually are; what an amount of remonstrance and resistance they sometimes encountered at the first. To take two or three Latin examples;—Cicero, in employing 'favor,' a word in a little while after used by everybody, does it with an apology, seems to feel that he is introducing a questionable novelty: 'urbanus,' too, in our sense of urbane, had in his time only just come up: 'obsequium' he believes Terence to have been the first to employ.* 'Soliloquium' seems to us so natural, indeed so necessary, a word, this 'soliloquy,' or talking of a man with himself alone, something which would so inevitably seek out its adequate expression, that it is with surprise we learn that no one spoke of 'soliloquy' before Augustine; the word having been invented, as he distinctly informs us, by himself.†

---

* On the new words in classical Latin see Quintilian, *Inst.* viii. 3, 30-37.   † *Solil.* 2. 7.

When a word has proved an unquestionable gain, it is interesting to watch it as it first comes forth, timid, and doubtful of the reception it will meet with; and the interest is much enhanced if it thus come forth on some memorable occasion, or from some memorable man. Both these interests meet in the word 'essay.' If it were demanded what is the most remarkable volume of essays which the world has seen, few, having sufficient oversight of the field of literature to be capable of replying, would fail to answer, Lord Bacon's. But they were also the first which bore that name; for we gather from the following passage in the (intended) dedication of the volume to Prince Henry, that 'essay' was itself a recent word in the language, and in the use to which he put it, perfectly novel: he says—' To write just treatises requireth leisure in the writer, and leisure in the reader; ... which is the cause which hath made me choose to write certain brief notes set down rather significantly than curiously, which I have called *Essays*. The word is late, but the thing is ancient.' From this dedication we gather that, little as 'essays' now can be considered a word of modesty, deprecating too large expectations on the part of the reader, it had, as 'sketches' perhaps would have now, as 'commentary' had in the Latin, that intention in its earliest use. In this deprecation of higher pretensions it resembled the 'philosopher' of Pythagoras. Others had styled themselves, or had been willing to be styled, 'wise men.' 'Lover of wisdom,' a name at once so modest and so beautiful, was of his devising.*

But while thus there are words which surprise us that they are so new, others surprise us that they are so old. Few, I should imagine, are aware that 'rationalist,' and this in a theological, and not merely a philosophical, sense, is of such early date as it is; or that we have not imported quite in these later times both the name and the thing from Germany. This is very far from the case. There was a sect of 'rationalists' in the time of the Commonwealth; and these challenging the name exactly on the same grounds as those who in later times have claimed it for their own. Thus, the author of a newsletter from London† among other things mentions: 'There is a new sect sprung up among them [the Presbyterians and Independents], and these are the *Rationalists*, and what their reason dictates them in Church or State stands for good, until they be convinced with better;' with more to the same effect. 'Christology' a reviewer has lately characterized as a monstrous importation from Germany. I am quite of his mind that English theology does not need, and can do excellently well without it; yet this novelty it is not; for in the *Preface* to the works of that illustrious Arminian divine of the seventeenth century, Thomas Jackson, written by Ben-

---

* Diogenes Laertius, *Proœm.* § 12.
† With date, Oct. 14, 1646; in *The Clarendon State Papers*, vol. ii. p. 40 of the *Appendix*.

jamin Oley, his friend and pupil, the following passage occurs: 'The reader will find in this author an eminent excellence in that part of divinity which I make bold to call *Christology*, in displaying the great mystery of godliness, God the Son manifested in human flesh.'*

In their power of taking up foreign words into healthy circulation and making them truly their own, languages differ much from one another, and the same language from itself at different periods of its life. There are languages of which the appetite and digestive power, the assimilative energy, is at some periods almost unlimited. Nothing is too hard for them; they will shape and mould to their own uses and habits almost any material offered to them. This, however, is in their youth; as age advances, this assimilative power diminishes. Words are still adopted; for this process of adoption can never wholly cease: but a chemical amalgamation of the new with the old does not any longer find place; or only in some instances, and very partially even in them. They lie upon the surface of the language; their sharp corners are not worn or rounded off; they remain foreign still in their aspect and outline, and, having missed their opportunity of becoming otherwise, will remain so to the end. Those who adopt, as with an inward misgiving about their own gift and power of stamping them afresh, make

---

* *Preface to Dr. Jackson's Works*, vol. i. p. xxvii. A work of Fleming's, published in 1700, bears the title, *Christology*.

a conscience of keeping them in exactly the same form in which they have received them; instead of conforming them to the laws of that new community into which they are now received. Nothing will illustrate this so well as a comparison of different words of the same family, which have at different periods been introduced into our language. We shall find that those of an earlier introduction have become English through and through, while the later introduced, belonging to the same group, have been very far from undergoing the same transforming process. Thus 'bishop,' a word as old as the introduction of Christianity into England, though not hiding its descent from 'episcopus,' is thoroughly English; while 'episcopal,' which has supplanted 'bishoply,' is only a Latin word in an English dress. 'Alms,' too, is genuine English, and English which has descended to us from far; the very shape in which we have the word, one syllable for 'eleëmosyna' of six, sufficiently testifying this; 'letters,' as Horne Tooke observes, 'like soldiers, being apt to desert and drop off in a long march.' The long and awkward 'eleëmosynary' is of far more recent date. Or sometimes this comparison is still more striking, when it is not merely words of the same family, but the very same word which has been twice adopted, at an earlier period and a later—the earlier form will be truly English, as 'palsy;' the latter will be only a Greek or Latin word spelt with English letters, as 'paralysis.' 'Dropsy,' 'quinsy,' 'megrim,' 'surgeon,' 'tansy,' 'dittany,' 'daffodil,' and many more words that one might name, have nothing of strangers or foreigners about them, have made themselves quite at home in English. So entirely is their physiognomy native, that it would be difficult even to suspect them to be of Greek descent, as they all are. Nor has 'kickshaws' anything about it now which would compel us at once to recognize in it the French 'quelques choses'*—'French *kickshose*,' as with allusion to the quarter from which it came, and while the memory of that was yet fresh in men's minds, it was often called by our early writers.

A notable fact about new words, and a very signal testimony of their birth from the bosom of the people, is the difficulty which is so often found in tracing their pedigree. When the *causæ vocum* are sought, which they justly are, and out of much more than mere curiosity, for the *causæ rerum* are very often contained in them, these continually elude research; and this, not merely where attention has only been called to the words, and interest about their etymology excited, long after they had been in popular use—for that words of a remote antiquity should often puzzle and perplex us, should give scope to idle guesses, or altogether defy conjecture, this is nothing strange—but even when it has been sought to investigate their origin

---

* 'These cooks have persuaded us their coarse fare is the best, and all other but what they dress to be mere *quelques choses*, made dishes of no nourishing' (Whitlock, *Zootomia*, p. 147).

almost as soon as they have come into existence. Their rise is mysterious; like so many acts of *becoming*, it is veiled in deepest obscurity. They appear, they are in everybody's mouth; but yet, when it is inquired from whence they are, nobody can tell. They are but of yesterday, and yet with inconceivable rapidity they have already forgotten the circumstances of their origin.

This rapidity with which words let go the secret of their origin is nowhere more striking than in the names of political or religious parties, and above all in the names of slight, of contempt, of scorn. Thus Baxter tells us in his most instructive *Narrative of his Life and Times*, that there already existed two explanations of 'Roundhead,'* a word not nearly so old as himself. How much has been written about the origin of the German 'Ketzer,' or heretic, which yet is still in debate; hardly less about the French 'cagot,' which however is pretty certainly '*canis Gothicus*,' this virtually excommunicated race being a real or supposed remnant of the refugee Gothic population of Spain among the Pyrenees. Is 'Lollard,' or 'Loller' as we have it in Chaucer, from 'lollen' to chaunt? that is, does it mean the chaunting or canting people? or had the Lollards their title from a principal person among them of this name,

---

* 'The original of which name is not certainly known. Some say it was because the Puritans then commonly wore short hair, and the king's party long hair: some say, it was because the Queen at Strafford's trial asked who that *round-headed* man was, meaning Mr. Pym, because he spake so strongly.' p. 34.

who suffered at the stake?—to say nothing of 'lolium' which some find in the name, these men being as *tares* among the wholesome wheat. The origin of 'Huguenot,' as applied to the French Protestants, was already a matter of doubt and discussion in the lifetime of those who first bore it.* Were the 'Waldenses' so called from one Waldus, to whom these 'Poor Men of Lyons,' as they were at first called, owed their origin? or is 'Waldenses' for Vallenses, the men of the Alpine valleys, the Dalesmen?—a question, the certain determination of which would go far to settle the most difficult and disputed points in the history of these witnesses for scriptural truth.

One might anticipate that a name like 'Canada,' given, and within fresh historic times, to a vast territory, would be accounted for; but it is not; so too that the Anglo-Americans would be able to explain how they got their word 'caucus,' which plays so prominent a part in their elections, but they cannot.† 'Cannibal' as a designation of man-eating savages, came first into use with the great discoveries in the western world of the fifteenth and sixteenth centuries; no certain explanation of it has yet been offered.‡ The Romans,

---

* Mahn (*Etymol. Untersuch.* p. 92) enumerates fifteen explanations which have been offered of the word.

† It is most probably a corruption of 'caulkers,' being derived from an association of these at Boston, who were especially active in preparing resistance to England in the period immediately preceding the War of Independence. The *thing* corresponds now very nearly to the Latin 'sodalicium.'

‡ Humboldt has certainly made it probable that 'canibal' (it

one might think, would be able to give some satisfactory account of the reason which moved them to call a subject region a 'province;' they are unfortunately able to give half a dozen reasons. Or once more, why were their 'catacombs' so called? Strange again that the Church should have lost the secret of 'Whit-Sunday' and whence it obtained its name; or, with all that we know now of the Middle Ages, that we do not know certainly the derivation of 'fief' and 'feudal.' Why the Roman military standard on which Constantine inscribed the symbols of the Christian faith should have been called 'Labarum' no one can tell. And yet the enquiry began early. A father of the Greek Church, almost a contemporary of Constantine, can do no more than suggest that 'labarum' is equivalent to 'laborum,' and that it was so called because in that victorious standard was the end of *labour* and toil (finis laborum)!*

Or take one word more, which has *not* lost the secret of its origin, in proof how easily it might lose this, and having once so done, how unlikely it would be that any searching would ever recover it. Burton tells us that the coarse cloth which is the medium of exchange in Eastern Africa, is called 'merkani.' The word is a native corruption of 'American,' the cloth being manufactured in

---

is spelt with a single n in all our early English) is a Latin corruption of 'Caribales,' a form under which Columbus designates the Caribs (propter rabiem *caninam* anthropophagorum gentis); as in French, 'appétit de *chien*.'

* Mahn, *Etym. Untersuch.* p. 65.

America and sold under this name. But suppose a change should take place in the country where this cloth was made, and it came little by little to be forgotten that it ever had been imported from America, who would then divine the secret of the word? Or, again, if the tradition of the etymology of 'paraffin' were once lost, it would be, I think, lost for ever. It is little likely that any mere ingenuity would divine the fact that a certain oil was so named because 'parum affinis,' having little affinity which chemistry could detect, with any other substance.

Those which I cited are but a handful of examples of the way in which words forget the circumstances of their birth. Now if we could believe in any merely *arbitrary* words, standing in connexion with nothing but the mere lawless caprice of some inventor, the impossibility of tracing their derivations would be nothing strange. Indeed it would be lost labour to seek for the parentage of all words, when many probably had none. But there is no such thing; there is no word which is not, as the Spanish gentleman loves to call himself, an 'hidalgo,' or son of something; if indeed this rendering of 'hidalgo' may stand. All are the embodiment, more or less successful, of a sensation, a thought, or a fact; or if of more fortuitous birth, still they attach themselves somewhere to the already subsisting world of words and things, and have their point of contact with it and departure from it, not always discoverable, as we see, but yet always existing.* And thus, when a word entirely refuses to give up the secret of its origin, it can be regarded in no other light but as a riddle which no one has succeeded in solving, a lock of which no man has found the key—but still a riddle which has a solution, a lock for which there is a key, though now, it may be, irrecoverably lost. And this difficulty, this impossibility oftentimes, of tracing the genealogy even of words of a very recent formation, is, as I observed, an evidence of the birth of the most vital of these out of the heart and from the lips of the people. Had they first appeared in books, something in the context would most probably explain them. Had they issued from the schools of the learned, these would not have failed to leave a recognizable stamp and mark upon them.

There is, indeed, another way in which obscurity may rest on a new word, or a word employed in a new sense; so that, while it offers no difficulty at all in its etymology, it may for all this offer difficulties in the explanation of that etymology almost or quite impossible to surmount. It may tell the story of its birth, of the word or words which compose it, may bear these on its front, so that none can mistake them, and yet the purpose and intention of the word may be hopelessly hidden from our eyes. The secret, having been once lost, is

---

* Some will remember here the old Greek dispute, whether words were θέσει or φύσει. It is needless to say that the last is the truth.

not again to be recovered. Thus no one has called,
or could call, in question the derivation of 'apocryphal,' that it means hidden away. When, however,
we begin to enquire why certain books which the
Church either set below the canonical Scriptures,
or rejected altogether, were called 'apocryphal,'
then a long and doubtful discussion commences.
Was it because their origin was *hidden* to the
early Fathers of the Church, and thus reasonable
suspicions of their authenticity entertained?* or
because they were mysteriously kept out of sight
and *hidden* by the heretical sects which boasted
themselves in their exclusive possession? or was
it that they were books not laid up in the Church
chest, but *hidden away* in obscure corners? or
were they books *worthier to be hidden* than to be
brought forward and read to the faithful?—for all
these explanations have been offered, and none
with such superiority of proof on its side as to
have put the others out of all right to be heard.
In the same way there is no question that 'tragedy'
is the song of the goat; but why this, whether
because a goat was the prize for the best performers of that song in which the germs of Greek
tragedy lay; or because the first actors were
dressed like satyrs in goatskins, is a question which
will now remain unsettled to the end. 'Leonine'
verses have plainly to do with 'leo' in some shape

---

* Augustine (*De Civ. Dei*, 15. 23): Apocrypha nuncupantur eo
quod eorum occulta origo non claruit Patribus. Cf. *Con. Faust.*
11. 2.

or other; but are they so called from one Leo or Leolinus, who first composed hexameters with this internal rhyme? or because, as the lion is king of beasts, so this, in the monkish estimation, was the king of metres? No one can certainly say. 'Sycophant' and 'superstition' are words, one in Greek and one in Latin, of the same character. No one doubts of what elements they are made up, and yet their secret has effectually been lost.*

But we must conclude. I may seem in this present lecture a little to have outrun your needs, and to have sometimes moved in a sphere too remote from that in which your future work will lie. And yet it is in truth very difficult to affirm of any words, that they do not touch us, do not in some way bear upon our studies, on that which we shall hereafter have to teach, or shall desire to learn; that there are any conquests which language makes that concern only a few, and may be regarded indifferently by all others. For it is here as with many inventions in the arts and luxuries of life; which, being at the first the exclusive privilege and possession of the wealthy and refined, gradually descend into lower strata of society, until at length what were once the elegancies and luxuries of a few, have become the decencies, well-nigh the necessities, of all. Not otherwise there are words, once only on the lips of philosophers or theologians, of the deeper

---

* For a good recapitulation of all which has been written on 'superstitio,' see Pott, *Etymol. Forsch.* 2nd ed., vol. ii. p. 921.

thinkers of their time, or of those interested in
their speculations, which step by step have come
down, not debasing themselves in this act of becoming popular, but training and elevating an
ever-increasing number to enter into their meaning, till at length they have become truly a part
of the nation's common stock, 'household words,'
used easily and intelligently by all.

I cannot better conclude this lecture than by
quoting a passage, one among many, which expresses with a rare eloquence all I have been
labouring to utter; for this truth, which many
have noticed, hardly any has set forth with
the same fulness of illustration, or the same
sense of its importance, as the author of *The
Philosophy of the Inductive Sciences*. 'Language,' he observes, 'is often called an instrument of thought, but it is also the nutriment
of thought; or rather, it is the atmosphere
in which thought lives; a medium essential to
the activity of our speculative powers, although
invisible and imperceptible in its operation; and
an element modifying, by its qualities and changes,
the growth and complexion of the faculties which
it feeds. In this way the influence of preceding
discoveries upon subsequent ones, of the past upon
the present, is most penetrating and universal,
although most subtle and difficult to trace. The
most familiar words and phrases are connected
by imperceptible ties with the reasonings and discoveries of former men and distant times. Their
knowledge is an inseparable part of ours; the

present generation inherits and uses the scientific wealth of all the past. And this is the fortune, not only of the great and rich in the intellectual world, of those who have the key to the ancient storehouses, and who have accumulated treasures of their own, but the humblest inquirer, while he puts his reasonings into words, benefits by the labours of the greatest. When he counts his little wealth, he finds he has in his hands coins which bear the image and superscription of ancient and modern intellectual dynasties, and that in virtue of this possession acquisitions are in his power, solid knowledge within his reach, which none could ever have attained to if it were not that the gold of truth once dug out of the mine circulates more and more widely among mankind.'

LECTURE VI.

ON THE DISTINCTION OF WORDS.

SYNONYMS and their distinction, with the advantages to be derived from their study, is the subject to which I shall next invite your attention. But what, you may ask, is meant, when, comparing certain words with one another, we affirm of them that they are synonyms? We mean that, with great and essential resemblances of meaning, they have at the same time small, subordinate, and partial differences—these differences being such as either originally, and on the ground of their etymology, inhered in them; or differences which they have by usage acquired; or such as, though nearly latent now, they are capable of receiving at the hands of wise and discreet masters of the tongue. Synonyms are words of like significance in the main, but with a certain unlikeness as well; with very much in common, but also with something private and particular, which they do not share with one another.*

---

* The word 'synonym' only found its way into the English language about the middle of the seventeenth century. Its incoming is marked by the Greek or Latin termination which for a while it bore; Jeremy Taylor writing 'synonymon,' Hacket 'synonymum,' and Milton (in the plural) 'synonyma.'

So soon as the term is defined thus, it will be at once perceived by any acquainted with the derivation, that, strictly speaking, it is a misnomer, and is given to words which fulfil these conditions in respect of one another with a certain inaccuracy and impropriety; since in strictness of speech the terms, 'synonyms,' or 'synonymous,' applied to words, affirm of them that they cover not merely almost, but altogether the same extent of meaning, that they are in their signification perfectly identical and coincident. The terms, however, are not ordinarily so used; they evidently are not so, when it is undertaken to trace out the distinction between synonyms; for, without venturing to deny that there may be such perfect synonyms, words, that is, with this absolute coincidence, yet these could not be the object of any such discrimination; since, where there was no real distinction, it would be lost labour and the exercise of a perverse ingenuity to attempt to draw one out.

There are, indeed, those who affirm that words in one language are never exactly synonymous, in all respects commensurate, with words in another; that, when they are compared, there is always something more or something less, or something different, which hinders this complete identity. And in respect of all words save those which designate objects in their nature absolutely incapable of a more or less, or of any qualitative difference, I should be disposed to consider the exceptions to this assertion exceedingly rare. For what, after all, is a word, but the enclosure of a certain district, larger or smaller, from the vast outfield of thought or fact, and in this a bringing of it into human cultivation, a redeeming of it for human uses? But how extremely unlikely it is that nations, drawing altogether independently of one another these lines of enclosure, should draw them in any cases exactly in the same direction, neither narrower nor wider; how inevitable, on the contrary, that very often the lines should not coincide—and this, even supposing no moral forces at work to disturb the falling of the lines. How immense and instructive a field of comparison between languages does this fact lay open to us; while it is sufficient to drive a translator with a high ideal of the task which he has undertaken well-nigh to despair.

Synonyms then, as the term is generally understood, and as I shall use it here, are words with slight differences already recognized between them, or with the capabilities of such. They are not on the one side words absolutely identical; but neither on the other side only remotely related to one another; for the differences between these last will be self-evident, will so lie on the surface and proclaim themselves to all, that it would be as superfluous an office as holding a candle to the sun to attempt to make this clearer than it already is. It may be desirable to fix the difference between scarlet and crimson; but between scarlet and green it would be absurd. They must be words which are more or less liable to confusion, but which yet ought not to be confounded; as one has said, 'quæ conjungi, non confundi, debent;' in which there originally inhered a difference, or between which, though once absolutely identical, such has gradually grown up, and so established itself in the use of the best writers, and in the instinct of the best speakers of the tongue, that it claims to be openly acknowledged by all.

But here an interesting question presents itself to us: How do languages come to possess synonyms of this latter class, which are differenced not by etymology nor by other deep-lying cause, but only by usage? Now if languages had been made by agreement, of course no such synonyms as these could exist; for when once a word had been found which was the adequate representative of a feeling or an object, no second one would have been sought. But languages are the result of processes very different from, and far less formal and regular than, this. Various tribes, each with its own dialect, kindred indeed, but in many respects distinct, coalesce into one people, and cast their contributions of language into a common stock. Thus the French possesses many synonyms from the *langue d'Oc* and *langue d'Oïl*, each having contributed its word for one and the same thing, as 'âtre' and 'foyer,' both for hearth. Sometimes two have the same word, but in forms sufficiently different to cause that both remain, but as different words; thus in Latin, 'serpo' and 'repo' are merely two slightly different formations of the same word; 'puteo' and 'fœteo' are the same; just as in German, 'Odem' and 'Athem' were only dialectic differences at the first. Or again, a conquering people have fixed themselves in the midst of a conquered; they impose their dominion, but do not succeed in imposing their language; nay, being few in number, they find themselves at last compelled to adopt the language of the conquered; or after a while that which may be called a transaction, a compromise between the two languages, finds place. One is adopted, but on the condition that it admits as naturalized denizens a vast number of the words of the other.

These are causes of the existence of synonyms, which reach far back into the history of a nation and a language; but other causes at a later period are also at work. When a written literature springs up, authors familiar with various foreign tongues, import from one and another words which are not absolutely required, which are oftentimes rather luxuries than necessities. Sometimes, having a very good word of their own, they must needs go and look for a finer one, as they esteem it, from abroad; as, for instance, the Latin having its own expressive 'succinum' (from 'succus'), for amber, some must import from the Greek the ambiguous 'electrum.' Of these thus proposed as candidates for admission, some fail to obtain the rights of citizenship, and after longer or shorter probation are rejected; it may be, never advance beyond their first proposer. Enough, however, receive the stamp of popular allowance to create embarrassment for a while, until, that is, their relations with the already existing words are adjusted. As a single illustration of the various quarters from which the English has thus been augmented and enriched, I would instance the words 'trick,' 'device,' 'finesse,' 'artifice,' and 'stratagem,' and enumerate the various sources from which we have drawn them. Here 'trick' is Saxon, 'devisa' is Italian, 'finesse' is French, 'artificium' is Latin, and 'stratagema' Greek.

By and by, however, as a language becomes itself an object of closer attention, at the same time that society, advancing from a simpler to a more complex state, has more things to designate, more thoughts to utter, and more distinctions to draw, it is felt a waste of resources to employ two or more words for the signifying of one and the same object. Men feel, and rightly, that with a boundless world lying around them and demanding to be named, and which they only make their own in the measure and to the extent that they do name it, with infinite shades and varieties of thought and feeling subsisting in their own minds, and claiming to find utterance in words, it is a mere and wanton extravagance to expend two or more signs on that which could adequately be set forth by one—an extravagance in one part of their expenditure, which will be almost sure to issue in, and to be punished by, a corresponding scantness and straitness in another. Some thought or feeling will wholly want its adequate sign, because another has two. Hereupon that which has been well called the process of 'desynonymizing' begins —that is, of gradually discriminating in use be-

tween words which have hitherto been accounted
perfectly equivalent, and, as such, indifferently
employed. It is a positive enriching of a language
when this process is at any point felt to be accomplished, when two or more words, once promiscuously used, have had each its own peculiar
domain assigned to it, which it shall not itself
overstep, upon which the others shall not encroach.
This may seem at first sight but as a better regula-
tion of old territory; for all practical purposes it
is the acquisition of new.

This desynonymizing process is not effected according to any prearranged purpose or plan. The
working genius of the language accomplishes its
own objects, causes these synonymous words insensibly to fall off from one another, and to acquire
separate and peculiar meanings. The most that
any single writer can do, save indeed in the terminology of science, is to assist an already existing
inclination, to bring to the consciousness of all
that which already has been implicitly felt by
many, and thus to hasten the process of this dis-
engagement, or, as it has been excellently expressed, 'to regulate and ordinate the evident nisus
and tendency of the popular usage into a severe
definition;' and establish on a firm basis the distinction, so that it shall not be lost sight of or
brought into question again. This, for instance,
Wordsworth did in respect of the words 'imagination' and 'fancy.' Before he wrote, it was, I
suppose, obscurely felt by most that in 'imagination' there was more of the earnest, in 'fancy' of

the play, of the spirit, that the first was a loftier faculty and gift than the second. The tendency of the language was in this direction. None would for some years back have employed 'fancy' as Milton employs it (*Paradise Lost*, v. 102-105), ascribing to it operations which we have learned to reserve for 'imagination' alone, and indeed subordinating 'imaginations' to it, as a part of the material with which it deals. Yet for all this the words were continually, and not without loss, confounded. Wordsworth first, in the *Preface* to his *Lyrical Ballads*, rendered it impossible for any, who had read and mastered what he had written on the two words, to remain unconscious any longer of the essential difference between them.*

* Thus De Quincey, *Letters to a Young Man whose Education has been neglected*: 'All languages tend to clear themselves of synonyms, as intellectual culture advances; the superfluous words being taken up and appropriated by new shades and combinations of thought evolved in the progress of society. And long before this appropriation is fixed and petrified, as it were, into the acknowledged vocabulary of the language, an insensible *clinamen* (to borrow a Lucretian word) prepares the way for it. Thus, for instance, before Mr. Wordsworth had unveiled the great philosophic distinction between the powers of *fancy* and *imagination*, the two words had begun to diverge from each other, the first being used to express a faculty somewhat capricious and exempted from law, the other to express a faculty more self-determined. When, therefore, it was at length perceived, that under an apparent unity of meaning there lurked a real dualism, and for philosophic purposes it was necessary that this distinction should have its appropriate expression, this necessity was met half way by the *clinamen* which had already affected the popular usage of the words.' Compare what Coleridge had before said, *Biogr. Lit.* vol. i. p. 90. It is to him we owe the word 'to desynonymize,'—against which, indeed, purists will object that it is

A multitude of words in English are still waiting for such a discrimination. Thus how real an ethical gain would it be, how much clearness would it bring into men's thoughts and feelings, if the distinction which exists in Latin between 'vindicta' and 'ultio,' that the first is a moral act, the just punishment of the sinner by his God, of the criminal by the judge, the other an act in which the self-gratification of one who counts himself injured or offended is sought, could in like manner be fully established (it does vaguely exist), between our 'vengeance' and 'revenge;' so that only 'vengeance' (with the verb 'avenge') should be ascribed to God, and to men acting as the executors of his righteous doom; while all in which their evil and sinful passions are the impulsive motive should be exclusively termed 'revenge.' As it now is, the moral disapprobation which cleaves, and cleaves justly, to 'revenge,' is oftentimes transferred almost unconsciously to 'vengeance;' while yet without vengeance it is impossible to conceive in an evil world any assertion of righteousness, any moral government whatsoever. These

---

of hyabrid formation, the prefix Latin, the body of the word Greek—and his own contributions direct and indirect in this province are perhaps both more and more important than those of any English writer; as, for instance, the disentanglement of 'fanaticism' and 'enthusiasm,' which we mainly owe to him (*Lit. Rem.* vol. ii. p. 385); of 'keenness' and 'subtilty' (*Table-Talk*, p. 140), 'poetry' and 'poesy' (*Lit. Rem.* vol. i. p. 219); 'analogy' and 'metaphor' (*Aids to Reflection*, p. 108. 1825); and that on which he himself laid so great a stress, 'reason' and 'understanding.'

distinctions which still wait to be made we may fitly regard as so much reversionary wealth in our mother tongue.

The causes mentioned above, that English, Anglo-Saxon in the main, yet draws so large a portion of its wealth from the Latin, and has further received, welcomed, and found place for many later additions, these have together effected that we possess in English a great many duplicates, not to speak of triplicates, or of such a quintuplicate as that which I adduced just now, where the Saxon, French, Italian, Latin, and Greek had each yielded us a word. Let me mention a few duplicate substantives, Anglo-Saxon and Latin: thus we have 'shepherd' and 'pastor;' 'feeling' and 'sentiment;' 'handbook' and 'manual;' 'ship' and 'nave;' 'anger' and 'ire;' 'grief' and 'dolour;' 'kingdom' and 'realm;' 'love' and 'charity;' 'feather' and 'plume;' 'forerunner' and 'precursor;' 'foresight' and 'providence;' 'freedom' and 'liberty;' 'murder' and 'homicide;' 'moons' and 'lunes;' —this last word is not met in the singular. Sometimes, in theology and science especially, we have gone both to the Latin and to the Greek, and drawn the same word from them both: thus 'deist' and 'theist;' 'numeration' and 'arithmetic;' 'Revelation' and 'Apocalypse;' 'temporal' and 'chronic;' 'compassion' and 'sympathy;' 'supposition' and 'hypothesis;' 'transparent' and 'diaphanous;' 'digit' and 'dactyle.' But to return to the Anglo-Saxon and Latin, the main factors of our tongue. Besides duplicate substantives, we have duplicate verbs, such as 'to heal' and 'to cure;' 'to whiten' and 'to blanch;' 'to soften' and 'to mollify;' 'to cloke' and 'to palliate;' with many more. Duplicate adjectives also are numerous, as 'shady' and 'umbrageous;' 'unreadable' and 'illegible;' 'unfriendly' and 'inimical;' 'almighty' and 'omnipotent.' Occasionally where only one substantive, an Anglo-Saxon, exists, yet the adjectives are duplicate, and the English, not adopting the Latin substantive, has admitted the adjective; thus 'burden' has not merely 'burdensome' but also 'onerous,' while yet 'onus' has found no place with us; 'priest' has 'priestly' and 'sacerdotal;' 'king' has 'kingly,' 'regal,' which is purely Latin, and 'royal,' which is Latin distilled through the Norman. 'Bodily' and 'corporal,' 'boyish' and 'puerile,' 'fiery' and 'igneous,' 'worldly' and 'mundane,' 'bloody' and 'sanguine,' 'watery' and 'aqueous,' 'fearful' and 'timid,' 'manly' and 'virile,' 'womanly' and 'feminine,' 'sunny' and 'solar,' 'starry' and 'stellar,' 'yearly' and 'annual,' 'wooden' and 'ligneous,' 'weighty' and 'ponderous,' may all be placed in the same list. Nor are these more than a handful of words out of the number which might be adduced; you would find both pleasure and profit in adding to these lists, and as far as you are able, making them gradually complete.

If we look closely at words which have succeeded in thus maintaining side by side their ground, we shall note that in almost every instance they have little by little asserted for themselves separate spheres of meaning, have in usage become more or less distinct. Thus we use 'shepherd' almost always in its primary meaning, keeper of sheep; while 'pastor' is exclusively used in the tropical sense, one that feeds the flock of God; at the same time the language having only the one adjective, 'pastoral,' that is of necessity common to both. 'Love' and 'charity' are used in our Authorized Version of Scripture promiscuously, and out of the sense of their equivalence are made to represent one and the same Greek word; but in modern use 'charity' has come predominantly to signify one particular manifestation of love, the supply of the bodily needs of others, 'love' continuing to express the affection of the soul. 'Ship' remains in its literal meaning, while 'nave' has become a symbolic term used in sacred architecture alone. 'Kingdom' is concrete, as the kingdom of Great Britain, 'reign' is abstract, the reign of Queen Victoria. 'Illegible' is applied to the handwriting, 'unreadable' to the subject-matter written; a man writes an 'illegible' hand; he has published an 'unreadable' book. 'Foresight' is ascribed to men, but 'providence' for the most part designates the far-looking wisdom of God, by which He governs and graciously cares for his people. It becomes boys to be 'boyish,' but not men to be 'puerile.' 'To blanch' is to withdraw colouring matter: we 'blanch' almonds or linen; or the cheek by the withdrawing of the blood is 'blanched' with fear; but we 'whiten' a wall, not by withdrawing some other colour, but by the superinducing of white; thus 'whited sepulchres.' When we 'palliate' our faults we do not seek 'to cloke' them altogether, but only to extenuate the guilt of them in part.

It might be urged that there was a certain preparedness in these words to separate off in their meaning from one another, inasmuch as they originally belonged to different stocks; and this may very well have assisted; but we find the same process at work where original difference of stock can have supplied no such assistance. 'Astronomy' and 'astrology' are both drawn from the Greek, nor is there any reason beforehand why the second should not be in as honourable use as the first; for it is the *reason*, as 'astronomy' the *law*, of the stars.* But seeing there is a true and a false science of the stars, both needing words to utter them, it has come to pass that in our later use, 'astrology' designates always that pretended science of imposture, which affecting to submit

---

* So entirely was any determining reason wanting, that for some while it was a question *which* word should obtain the honourable employment, and it seemed as if 'astrology' and 'astrologer' would have done so, as this extract from Bishop Hooper makes abundantly plain (*Early Writings*, Parker Society ed., p. 331): 'The *astrologer* is he that knoweth the course and motions of the heavens and teacheth the same; which is a virtue if it pass not his bounds, and become of an astrologer an *astronomer*, who taketh upon him to give judgment and censure of these motions and courses of the heavens, what they prognosticate and destiny unto the creature.'

the moral freedom of men to the influences of the heavenly bodies, prognosticates future events from the position of these, as contrasted with 'astronomy,' that true science which investigates the laws of the heavenly bodies in their relations to one another and to the planet upon which we dwell.

As these are both from the Greek, so 'despair' and 'diffidence' are both, though the second more directly than the first, from the Latin. At a period not very long past the difference between them was hardly appreciable; one was hardly stronger than the other. If in one the absence of all *hope*, in the other that of all *faith*, was implied. In *The Pilgrim's Progress*, a book with which every English schoolmaster will be familiar, 'Mistress *Diffidence*' is 'Giant *Despair's*' wife, and not a whit behind him in deadly enmity to the pilgrims; even as Jeremy Taylor speaks of the impenitent sinner's '*diffidence* in the hour of death,' meaning, as the context plainly shows, his despair. But to what end two words for one and the same thing? And thus 'diffidence' did not retain that energy of meaning which it had at the first, but little by little assumed a more mitigated sense, (Hobbes speaks of 'men's diffidence,' or distrust 'of one another,') till it has come now to signify a becoming distrust of ourselves, a humble estimate of our own powers, with only a slight intimation, as in the later use of the Latin 'verecundia,' that perhaps this distrust is carried too far.

Again, 'interference' and 'interposition' are both from the Latin; and here too there is no anterior necessity that they should possess those different shades of meaning which yet they have obtained among us;—the Latin verbs which form their latter halves being about as strong one as the other. And yet in our practical use, 'interference' is something offensive; it is the pushing in of himself between two parties on the part of a third, who was not asked, and is not thanked for his pains, and who, as the feeling of the word implies, had no business there; while 'interposition' is employed to express the friendly peace-making mediation of one whom the act well became, and who, even if he was not specially invited thereunto, is still thanked for what he has done. How real an increase is it in the wealth and efficiency of a language thus to have discriminated such words as these; and to be able to express acts outwardly the same by different words, according as we would praise them or blame.*

---

* If in the course of time distinctions are thus created, and if this is the tendency of language, yet they are also sometimes, though far less often, obliterated. Thus the fine distinction between 'yea' and 'yes,' 'nay' and 'no,' once existing in English, has quite disappeared. 'Yea' and 'Nay,' in Wiclif's time, and a good deal later, were the answers to questions framed in the affirmative. 'Will he come?' To this it would have been replied, 'Yea' or 'Nay,' as the case might be. But 'Will he not come?'—to this the answer would have been, 'Yes' or 'No.' Sir Thomas More finds fault with Tyndale, that in his translation of the Bible he had not observed this distinction, which was evidently therefore going out even then, that is in the reign of Henry VIII., and shortly after it was quite forgotten.

Take now some words not thus desynonymized by usage only, but having an inherent etymological distinction,—one, however, which it might be easy to overlook, which, so long as we dwell on the surface of the word, we shall overlook; and see whether we shall not be gainers by bringing out the distinction into clear consciousness. Here are 'arrogant,' 'presumptuous,' and 'insolent;' we often use them promiscuously; yet let us examine them a little more closely, and ask ourselves, as soon as we have traced the lines of demarcation between them, whether we are not now in possession of three distinct thoughts, instead of a single confused one. He is 'arrogant,' who claims the observance and homage of others as his due (ad rogo); who does not wait for them to offer, but himself demands all this; or who, having right to one sort of observance, claims another to which he has no right. Thus, it was 'arrogance' in Nebuchadnezzar, when he required that all men should fall down before the image which he had reared. He, a man, was claiming for man's work the homage which belonged only to God. But one is 'presumptuous' who *takes* things to himself *before* he has acquired any title to them (præ sumo); as the young man who already takes the place of the old, the learner who speaks with the authority of the teacher. By and by all this may very justly be his, but it is 'presumption' to anticipate it now. 'Insolent' means properly no more than unusual; to act 'insolently' is to act unusually. The offensive sense which 'insolent' has acquired rests upon the feeling that there is a certain well-understood rule of society, a recognized standard of moral behaviour, to which each of its members should conform. The 'insolent' man is one who violates this rule, who breaks through this order, acting in an *unaccustomed* manner. The same sense of the orderly being also the moral, is implied in 'irregular;' a man of 'irregular,' is for us a man of immoral, life; and yet more strongly in the Latin language, which has but one word (mores) for customs and morals.

Or consider the following words: 'to hate,' 'to loathe,' 'to detest,' and 'to abhor.' Each of them rests on an image entirely distinct from the others; two, the first and second, being Anglo-Saxon, and the others Latin. 'To hate' is properly to be *inflamed* with passionate dislike, the word being connected with 'heat,' 'hot;' just as we speak, using the same figure, of persons being 'incensed' with anger, or of their anger 'kindling;' 'ira' and 'uro' being perhaps in like manner related; and 'excandescentia' at any rate resting on this same image. 'To loathe' is properly to feel nausea, the turning of the stomach at that which excites first natural, and then by a transfer, moral disgust. 'To detest' is to bear witness against, not to be able to keep silence in regard of something, to feel ourselves obliged to lift up our voice and testimony against it. 'To abhor' is to shrink shuddering back, as one would from an object of fear, a hissing serpent rising in one's path. Thus our blessed Lord 'hated' to see his

Father's house profaned, when, the zeal of that house consuming Him, He drove forth in anger the profaners from it (John ii. 15); He 'loathed' the lukewarmness of the Laodiceans, when He threatened to spue them out of his mouth (Rev. iii. 16); He 'detested' the hypocrisy of the Pharisees and Scribes, when He proclaimed their sin, and uttered those eight woes against them (Matt. xxiii.); He 'abhorred' the evil suggestions of Satan, when He bade the Tempter to get behind Him, seeking to put a distance between Himself and him (Matt. iv. 10).

Sometimes words have no right at all to be considered synonyms, and yet are constantly used one for the other; having in fact more need than synonyms themselves to be discriminated. Thus, what confusion is often made between 'genuine' and 'authentic;' what inaccuracy exists in their use. And yet the distinction is a very plain one. A 'genuine' work is one written by the author whose name it bears; an 'authentic' work is one which relates truthfully the matters of which it treats. For example, the apocryphal *Gospel of St. Thomas* is neither 'genuine' nor 'authentic.' It is not 'genuine,' for St. Thomas did not write it; it is not 'authentic,' for its contents are mainly fables and lies. The history of the Alexandrian War, which goes under Cæsar's name, is not 'genuine,' for he did not write it; it is 'authentic,' being in the main a truthful record of the events which it professes to relate. Thiers' *History of the French Empire*, on the contrary, is 'genuine,' for he is certainly the author, but very far from 'authentic;' while Thucydides' *History of the Peloponnesian War* is 'authentic' and 'genuine' both.

You will observe that in most of the words just adduced, I have sought to refer their usage to their etymologies, to follow the guidance of these, and by the same aid to trace the lines of demarcation which divide them. For I cannot but think it an omission in a very instructive volume upon synonyms edited by the late Archbishop Whately, and a partial diminution of its usefulness, that in the valuation of words reference is so seldom made to these, the writer relying almost entirely on present usage, and the tact and instinct of a cultivated mind for the appreciation of them aright. The accomplished author (or authoress) of this book indeed justifies this omission on the ground that a book of synonyms has to do with the present relative value of words, not with their roots and derivations; and further, that a reference to these brings in often what is only a disturbing force in the process, tending to confuse rather than to clear.* But while it is quite true that

---

* Among words whose etymology might mislead as to their present meaning, the writer adduces 'allegiance,' which by usage signifies 'the fidelity of the subject to his prince,' while the etymology would rather suggest 'conformity to law.' But surely to derive it from 'ad legem,' is an error; it is rather from 'alligo,' as 'liege' from 'ligo;' and thus is perfectly true to its etymology, signifying the obligation wherewith one is bound to his superior. Algernon Sidney (*Discourse concerning Government*, c. iii. § 36) falls into the same mistake; who, replying to some

words may often ride very slackly at anchor on their etymologies, may be borne hither and thither by the shifting tides and currents of usage, yet are they for the most part still holden by them. Very few have broken away and drifted from their moorings altogether. A 'novelist,' or writer of *new* tales in the present day is very different from a 'novelist' or upholder of *new* theories in politics and religion, of two hundred years ago; yet the idea of *newness* is common to them both. A 'naturalist' was then a denier of revealed truth, of any but *natural* religion; he is now an investigator, he is often a devout one, of *nature* and of her laws; yet the word has remained true to its etymology all the while. A 'methodist' was once a follower of a certain 'method' of philosophical induction, now of a 'method' in the fulfilment of religious duties; but in either case 'method,' or orderly progression, is the soul of the word. Take other words which have changed or modified their meaning—'plantations,' for instance, which were once colonies of men, (and indeed we still 'plant' a colony,) but are now nurseries of young trees, and you will find the

---

who maintained that submission was due to kings, even though these should violate the fundamental laws of the state, observes that the very word 'allegiance,' of which they made so much, refuted them; for this was plainly 'such an obedience as the law requires.' He would have done better to appeal to the word 'loyalty,' which expresses properly that fidelity which one owes according to *law*, and does not necessarily include that attachment to the royal person, which happily we in England have been able further to throw into the word.

same to hold good. 'Ecstasy' *was* madness, it *is* intense delight; but in neither case has it departed from its fundamental meaning, since it is the nature alike of this and that *to set men out of and beside themselves.*

And even when the fact is not so obvious as in these cases, the etymology of a word exercises an unconscious influence upon its uses, oftentimes makes itself felt when least expected, so that a word, after seeming quite to have forgotten, will after longest wanderings, return to it again. And one of the arts of a great poet or prose writer, who wishes to add emphasis to his style, to bring out all the latent forces of his native tongue, will very often consist in reconnecting a word by his use of it with its original derivation, in not suffering it to forget itself and its origin, though it would. How often and with what signal effect Milton does this; while yet how often the fact that he is doing it passes even by scholars unobserved.* And even if all this were not so, yet the

---

* I will give in a note a few illustrations of this his manner of dealing with words. And let me observe that any one who desires, as he reads Milton, really to understand him, will do well to be ever on the watch for such recalling upon his part, of words to their primitive sense; and as often as he detects, to make accurate note of it for his own use, and, so far as he is a teacher, for the use of others. Take a few examples out of many; 'ambition' (*P. L.* i. 262; *S. A.* 247); 'astonished' (*P. L.* i. 266); 'pomp' (*P. L.* viii. 61); 'chaos' (*P. L.* vi. 55); 'seditious' (*P. L.* vi. 152); 'diamond' (*P. L.* vi. 364); 'extenuate' (*P. L.* x. 645); 'implicit' (*P. L.* vii. 323); 'indorse' (*P. R.* iii. 329); 'empiric' (*P. L.* v. 440); 'secular' (*S. A.* 1707); 'sagacious' (*P. L.* x. 281); 'transact' (*P. L.* vi. 286).

past history of a word, which history must needs *start* from its derivation, how soon soever that may be left behind, is surely a necessary element in its present valuation. What Barrow says is quite true, that 'knowing the primitive meaning of words can seldom or never *determine* their meaning anywhere, they often in common use declining from it;' but though it cannot determine, it can as little be left safely out of sight, when this determination is being made. A man may be wholly different now from what once he was, yet not the less to know his antecedents is needful, before we can ever perfectly understand his present self; and the same holds good with a word.

There is often a moral value in the possession of synonyms, enabling us, as they do, to say exactly what we intend, without exaggerating or the putting of more into our words than we feel in our hearts, allowing us, as one has said, to be at once courteous and precise. Such moral advantage there is, for example, in the choice which we have between the words 'to felicitate' and 'to congratulate,' for the expressing of our sentiments and wishes in regard of the good fortune that happens to others. 'To felicitate' another is to wish him happiness, without affirming that his happiness is also ours. Thus, out of that general goodwill with which we ought to regard all, we might 'felicitate' one almost a stranger to us; nay, more, I can honestly 'felicitate' one on his appointment to a post, or attainment of an honour, even though I may not consider him the fittest to have obtained it, though I should have been glad if another had done so; I can desire and hope, that is, that it may bring all joy and happiness to him. But I could not, without a violation of truth, 'congratulate' him, or that stranger whose prosperity awoke no lively delight in my heart; for when I 'congratulate' a person (con gratulor), I declare that I am sharer in his joy, that what has rejoiced him has rejoiced also me. We have all, I dare say, felt, even without having analysed the distinction between the words, that 'congratulate' is a far heartier word than 'felicitate,' and one with which it much better becomes us to welcome the good fortune of a friend; and the analysis, as you perceive, perfectly justifies the feeling. 'Felicitations' are little better than compliments; 'congratulations' are the expression of a genuine sympathy and joy.

Let me illustrate the importance of synonymous distinctions by another example, by the words, 'to invent' and 'to discover;' or 'invention' and 'discovery.' How slight may seem to us the distinction between them, even if we see any at all. Yet try them a little closer, try them, which is the true proof, by aid of examples, and you will perceive that by no means can they be indifferently used; that, on the contrary, a great principle lies at the root of their distinction. Thus we speak of the 'invention' of printing, of the 'discovery' of America. Shift these words, and speak, for instance, of the 'invention' of

America; you feel at once how unsuitable the language is. And why? Because Columbus did not make that to be, which before him had not been. America was there, before he revealed it to European eyes; but that which before *was*, he *showed* to be; he withdrew the veil which hitherto had concealed it; he 'discovered' it. So too we speak of Newton 'discovering' the law of gravitation; he drew aside the veil whereby men's eyes were hindered from perceiving it, but the law had existed from the beginning of the world, and would have existed whether he or any other man had traced it or no; neither was it in any way affected by the discovery of it which he had made. But Gutenburg, or whoever else it may have been to whom the honour belongs, 'invented' printing; he made something to be, which hitherto was not. In like manner Harvey 'discovered' the circulation of the blood; but Watt 'invented' the steam-engine; and we speak, with a true distinction, of the 'inventions' of Art, the 'discoveries' of Science. In the very highest matters of all, it is deeply important that we be aware of and observe the distinction. In religion there have been many 'discoveries,' but (in true religion I mean) no 'inventions.' Many discoveries—but God in each case the discoverer; He draws away the veils, one veil after another, that have hidden Him from men; the discovery or revelation is from Himself, for no man by searching has found out God; and therefore, wherever anything offers itself as an 'invention' in matters of religion, it proclaims itself a lie,—all self-devised worships, all religions which man projects from his own heart. Just that is known of God which He is pleased to make known, and no more; and men's recognizing or refusing to recognize in no way affects it. They may deny or may acknowledge Him, but He continues the same.

As involving in like manner a distinction which cannot safely be lost sight of, how important the difference, of which the existence is asserted by our possession of the two words, 'to apprehend' and 'to comprehend,' with their substantives, 'apprehension' and 'comprehension.' For indeed we 'apprehend' many truths, which we do not 'comprehend.' The great mysteries of our faith—the doctrine for instance of the Holy Trinity, we lay hold upon it (*ad* prehendo), we hang on it, our souls live by it; but we do not '*com*prehend' it, that is, we do not take it all in; for it is a necessary attribute of God that He is *incomprehensible*; if He were not so, either He would not be God, or the being that comprehended Him would be God also. But it also belongs to the idea of God that He may be '*a*pprehended,' though not '*com*prehended,' by His reasonable creatures; He has made them to know Him, though not to know Him *all*, to '*a*pprehend,' though not to '*com*prehend' Him. We may transfer with profit the same distinction to matters not quite so solemn. I read Goldsmith's *Traveller*, or one of Gay's *Fables*, and I feel that I 'comprehend' it;—I do not believe, that is, that there was any thing in the poet's mind or intention, which I have not in the reading reproduced in my own. But I read *Hamlet*, or *King Lear*: here I 'apprehend' much; I have wondrous glimpses of the poet's intention and aim; but I do not for an instant suppose that I have 'comprehended,' taken in, that is, all that was in his mind in the writing; or that his purpose does not stretch in manifold directions far beyond the range of my vision; and I am sure there are few who would not shrink from affirming, at least if they at all realized the force of the words they were using, that they 'comprehended' Shakespeare; however much they may 'apprehend' in him.

How often 'opposite' and 'contrary' are used as if there was no difference between them, and yet there is a most essential one, one which perhaps we may best express by saying that 'opposites' complete, while 'contraries' exclude one another. Thus the most 'opposite' moral or mental characteristics may meet in one and the same person, while to say that the most 'contrary' did so, would be manifestly absurd; for example, a soldier may be at once prudent and bold, for these are opposites; he could not be at once prudent and rash, for these are contraries. We may love and fear at the same time and the same person; we pray in the Litany that we may love and fear God, the two being opposites, and thus the complements of one another; but to pray that we might love and hate would be as illogical as it would be impious, for these are contraries, and

could no more coexist together than white and
black, hot and cold, in the same subject at the
same time. Or to take another illustration, sweet
and sour are 'opposites,' sweet and bitter are
'contraries.' * It will be seen then that there is
always a certain relation between 'opposites;'
they unfold themselves though in different directions from the same root, as the positive and
negative forces of electricity, and in their very
opposition uphold and sustain one another; while
'contraries' encounter one another from quarters
quite diverse, and one only subsists in the exact
degree that it puts out of working the other.
Surely this distinction cannot be an unimportant
one either in the region of ethics or elsewhere.

It will happen continually that rightly to distinguish between two words will throw a flood of
light upon some controversy in which they play
a principal part, nay, may virtually put an end
to that controversy altogether. Thus when
Hobbes, with a true instinct, would have laid
deep the foundations of atheism and despotism
together, resolving all right into might, and not
merely robbing men, if he could, of the power,
but denying to them the duty, of obeying God
rather than man, his sophisms could stand only
so long as it was not perceived that 'compulsion'
and 'obligation,' with which he juggled, conveyed
two ideas perfectly distinct, indeed disparate, in
kind. Those sophisms of his collapsed at once, so

---

* See Coleridge, *Church and State*, p. 18.

soon as it was perceived that what pertained to one had been transferred to the other by a mere confusion of terms and cunning sleight of hand, the former being a *physical*, the latter a *moral* necessity.

There is indeed no such fruitful source of confusion and mischief as this—two words are tacitly assumed as equivalent, and therefore exchangeable, and then that which may be assumed, and with truth, of one, is assumed also of the other, of which it is not true. Thus, for instance, it often is with 'instruction' and 'education.' Cannot we 'instruct' a child, it is asked, cannot we teach it geography, or arithmetic, or grammar, quite independently of the Catechism, or even of the Scriptures? No doubt you may; but can you 'educate,' without bringing moral and spiritual forces to bear upon the mind and affections of the child? And you must not be permitted to transfer the admissions which we freely make in regard of 'instruction,' as though they also held good in respect of 'education.' For what is 'education'? Is it a furnishing of a man from without with knowledge and facts and information? or is it a drawing forth from within and a training of the spirit, of the true humanity which is latent in him? Is the process of education the filling of the child's mind, as a cistern is filled with waters brought in buckets from some other source? or the opening up for that child of fountains which are already there? Now if we give any heed to the word 'education,' and to the voice which speaks

in the word, we shall not long be in doubt.
Education must educe, being from 'educare,'
which is but another form of 'educere;' and that
is to draw out, and not to put in. 'To draw out'
what is in the child, the immortal spirit which is
there, this is the end of education; and so much
the word declares. The putting in is indeed
most needful, that is, the child must be instructed
as well as educated, and 'instruction' means
furnishing; but not instructed instead of educated.
He must first have powers awakened in him,
measures of spiritual value given him; and then
he will know how to deal with the facts of this
outward world; then instruction in these will
profit him; but not without the higher training,
still less as a substitute for it.

It has occasionally happened that the question
which out of two apparent synonyms should be
adopted in some important state-document has
been debated with no little earnestness and
vigour; as at the great English Revolution of
1688, when the two Houses of Parliament were
at issue whether it should be declared of James
the Second that he had 'abdicated,' or 'deserted,'
the throne. This might seem at first sight a
mere strife about words, and yet, in reality, serious
constitutional questions were involved in the
debate. The Commons insisted on the word
'abdicated,' not as wishing to imply that in any
act of the late king there had been an official
renunciation of the crown, which would have
been manifestly untrue; but because 'abdicated'

to their minds alone expressed the fact that James had so borne himself as virtually to have entirely renounced, disowned, and relinquished the crown, to have irrecoverably forfeited and separated himself from it, and from any right to it for ever; while 'deserted' would have seemed to leave room and an opening for a return, which they were determined to declare for ever excluded; as, were it said of a husband that he had 'deserted' his wife, or of a soldier that he had 'deserted' his colours, this language would imply not only that he might, but that he was bound to return. Lord Somers' speech on the occasion is a masterly specimen of synonymous discrimination, and an example of the uses in highest matters of state to which it may be turned. As little was it a mere strife about words when at the restoration of our interrupted relations with Persia, Lord Palmerston insisted that the Shah should address the Queen of England not as 'Malckelh' but as 'Padischah,' refusing to receive letters which wanted this superscription.

Let me press upon you in conclusion some few of the many advantages to be derived from the habit of distinguishing synonyms. These advantages we might presume to be many, even though we could not ourselves perceive them; for how often do the great masters of style in every tongue, perhaps none so often as Cicero, the greatest of all,* pause to discriminate between

---

* Thus he distinguishes between 'voluntas' and 'cupiditas;' 'cautio' and 'metus' (*Tusc.* 4. 6); 'gaudium,' 'lætitia,' 'vo-

the words they are using; how much care and
labour, how much subtlety of thought, they have
counted well bestowed on the operation; how
much importance do they avowedly attach to it;
not to say that their works, even where they do
not intend it, will be a continual lesson in this
respect: a great writer merely in the accuracy
with which he employs words will always be exer-
cising us in synonymous distinction. But the
advantages of attending to synonyms need not be
taken on trust; they are evident. How large a
part of true wisdom it is to be able to distinguish
between things that differ, things seemingly, but

---

luptas' (*Tusc.* 4. 6; *Fin.* 2. 4); 'prudentia' and 'sapientia' (*Off.*
1. 43); 'caritas' and 'amor' (*De Part. Or.* 25); 'ebrius' and
'ebriosus,' 'iracundus' and 'iratus,' 'anxietas' and 'angor'
(*Tusc.* 4. 12); 'vitium,' 'morbus,' 'aegrotatio' (*Tusc.* 4. 13);
'labor' and 'dolor' (*Tusc.* 2. 15); 'furor' and 'insania' (*Tusc.*
3. 5); 'malitia' and 'vitiositas' (*Tusc.* 4. 15). Quintilian
also often bestows attention on synonyms, observing well (vi. 3.
17); 'Pluribus nominibus in eâdem re vulgo utimur; quæ
tamen si diducas, suam quandam propriam vim ostendent:' he
adduces 'salsum,' 'urbanum,' 'facetum,' 6. 3. Among Church
writers Augustine is a frequent and successful discriminator of
words. Thus he separates off from one another 'flagitium' and
'facinus' (*De Doct. Christ.* 3. 10); 'æmulatio' and 'invidia'
(*Expl. ad Gal.* v. 20); 'arrha' and 'pignus' (*Serm.* 23. 8, 9);
'studiosus' and 'curiosus' (*De Util. Cred.* 9); 'sapientia' and
'scientia;' (*De Div. Quæst.* 2. qu. 2); 'senecta' and 'senium'
(*Enarr. in Ps.* 70. 18): 'schisma' and 'hæresis' (*Con. Cresc.*
2. 7); with many more. Among the merits of Grimm's German Dictionary is the care which he bestows on the discrimination of synonyms, as between 'Degen' and 'Schwert;' 'Felde'
'Acker' and 'Heide;' 'Aar' and 'Adler;' 'Antlitz' and
'Angesicht;' 'Kelch' 'Becher' and 'Glas,' 'Frau' and 'Weib;
'Butter' 'Schmalz' and 'Anke.'

not really, alike, this is remarkably attested by our words 'discernment' and 'discretion;' which are now used as equivalent, the first to 'insight,' the second to 'prudence;' while yet in their earlier usage, and according to their etymology, being both from 'discerno,' they signify the power of so seeing things that in the seeing we distinguish and separate them one from another.*
Such were originally 'discernment' and 'discretion,' and such in great measure they are still. And in words is a material ever at hand on which to train the spirit to a skilfulness in this; on which to exercise its sagacity through the habit of distinguishing there where it would be so easy to confound. Nor is this habit of discrimination only valuable as a part of our intellectual training; but what a positive increase is it of mental wealth when we have learned to discern between things, which really differ, but have been hitherto confused in our minds; and have made these distinctions permanently our own in the only way by which they can be made secure, that is, by assigning to each its appropriate word and peculiar sign.

In the effort to trace lines of demarcation you may little by little be drawn into the heart of subjects the most instructive; for only as you have thoroughly mastered a subject, and all which is most characteristic about it, can you hope to trace

---

* 'L'esprit consiste à connaître la ressemblance des choses diverses, et la différence des choses semblables' (Montesquieu).

these lines with accuracy and success. A Roman might bear four names: 'prænomen,' 'nomen,' 'cognomen,' 'agnomen;' almost always bore three. You will know something of Roman life when you can tell the exact story of each of these, and the precise difference between them. He will not be altogether ignorant of the Middle Ages, and of the clamps which in them bound society together, who has learned thoroughly to distinguish between a 'fief' and a 'benefice.'. He will have obtained a firm grasp on some central facts of theology who can exactly draw out the distinction between 'reconciliation,' 'propitiation,' 'atonement,' as used in the New Testament; in Church History, who can trace the difference between a 'schism' and a 'heresy.' One who has learned to discriminate between 'detraction' and 'slander,' as Barrow has done before him, or between 'emulation' and 'envy,' in which South has excellently shown him the way,[*] or between 'avarice' and 'covetousness,' will not have made an unprofitable excursion into the region of ethics.

How important a help, moreover, will it prove to the writing of a good English style, if instead of choosing almost at hap-hazard from a group of words which seem to us one about as fit for our purpose as an other, we at once know which, and which only, we ought in the case before us to employ, which will be the exact vesture of our thoughts. It is the first characteristic of a well-

---

[*] *Sermons*, 1737, vol. v. p. 403.

dressed man that his clothes fit him: they are not too small and shrunken here, too large and loose there. Now it is precisely such a prime characteristic of a good style that the words fit close to the thoughts: they will not be too big here, hanging like a giant's robe on the limbs of a dwarf; nor too small there, as a boy's garments into which the man has painfully and ridiculously thrust himself. You do not feel in one place that the writer means more than he has succeeded in saying; in another that he has said more than he means; or in a third something beside what his intention was; and all this, from a lack of dexterity in employing the instrument of language, of precision in knowing what words would be the exactest correspondents and fittest exponents of his thoughts.*

What unemployed wealth in almost every language exists, certainly not least in our own. How much of what might be as its current coin, is shut up in the treasure-house of a few classical authors, or is never to be met with at all but in the pages of our dictionaries—we meanwhile in the midst of all this riches adjudging ourselves to a voluntary poverty, and often with work the most delicate and difficult to accomplish, for surely the clothing of thought in its most appropriate

---

* 'La propriété des termes est le caractère distinctif des grands écrivains; c'est par là que leur style est toujours au niveau de leur sujet; c'est à cette qualité qu'on reconnaît le vrai talent d'écrire, et non à l'art futile de déguiser par un vain coloris les idées communes' (D'Alembert).

garment of words is this, needlessly depriving
ourselves of a large portion of the helps at our
command; like some workman who, being provided for an operation that will task all his
skill with a dozen different tools, each adapted for
its own special work, should in his indolence and
self-conceit persist in using only one; doing
coarsely what might have been done finely; or
leaving altogether undone what, with these assistances, was quite within his reach. And thus
it comes to pass that in the common intercourse
of life, often too in books, a certain number
of words are worked almost to death, employed in
season and out of season—a vast multitude meanwhile being rarely, if at all, called to render the
service which they could render better than any
other; so rarely, that little by little they slip out
of sight and are forgotten. And then, perhaps, at
some later day, when their want is felt, the ignorance in which we have allowed ourselves of the
resources offered by the language to satisfy the
demands of thought, sends us abroad in search of
outlandish substitutes for words which we already
possess at home.

And let us not suppose the power of exactly
saying what we mean, and neither more nor less
than we mean, to be merely an elegant mental
accomplishment. It is indeed this, and perhaps
there is no power so surely indicative of a high
and accurate training of the intellectual faculties.
But it is also much more than this: it has a
moral value as well. It is nearly allied to

morality, inasmuch as it is nearly connected with truthfulness. Every man who has himself in any degree cared for the truth, and occupied himself in seeking it, is more or less aware how much of the falsehood in the world passes current under the concealment of words, how many strifes and controversies,

'Which feed the simple, and offend the wise,'

find all or nearly all their fuel and their nourishment in words carelessly or dishonestly employed. And when a man has had any actual experience of this, and at all perceived how far this mischief reaches, he is sometimes almost tempted to say with Shakespeare's clown, ' Words are grown so false, I am loath to prove reason with them.' He cannot, however, forego their employment; not to say that he will presently perceive that this falseness of theirs whereof he accuses them, this cheating power of words, is not of their proper use, but only of their abuse; he will see that, however they may have been enlisted in the service of lies, they are yet of themselves most true; and that where the bane is, there the antidote should be sought as well. If Goethe's Faust denounces words and the falsehood of words, it is by the aid of words that he does so. Ask then words what they mean, that you may deliver yourselves, that you may help to deliver others, from the tyranny of words, and from the strife of ' word-warriors.' Learn to distinguish between them, for you have the authority of Hooker, that ' the mixture of those things by speech, which by nature are divided, is the mother of all error.' And although I cannot promise you that the study of synonyms, or the acquaintance with derivatives, or any other knowledge but the very highest knowledge of all, will deliver you from the temptation to misuse this or any other gift of God—a temptation which always lies so near us—yet I am sure that these studies rightly pursued will do much in leading us to stand in awe of this gift of words, and to tremble at the thought of turning it to any other than those worthy ends for which God has endowed us with a faculty so divine.

LECTURE VII.

THE SCHOOLMASTER'S USE OF WORDS.

SOME years ago, namely, at the Great Exhibition of 1851, there might be seen a collection, probably by far the completest which has ever been got together, of what were called *the material helps of education*. There was then gathered in a single room all the outward machinery of moral and intellectual training; all by which order might be best maintained, the labour of the teacher and the taught economised, with a thousand ingenious devices suggested by the best experience of many minds, and of these during many years. Nor were these material helps of education merely mechanical. There were in that collection vivid representations of places and objects; models which often preserved their actual forms and proportions, not to speak of maps and of books. No one who is aware how much in schools, and indeed everywhere else, depends on what apparently is slight and external, would undervalue the helps and hints which such a collection would furnish to many. And yet it would be well for us to remember that even if we were to obtain all this apparatus in its completest

form, and possessed the most perfect skill in its
application, so that it should never encumber but
always assist us, we should yet have obtained very
little compared to that which as a help to education is already ours. When we stand face to face
with a child, that word which the child possesses
in common with ourselves is a far more potent
implement and aid of education than all these external helps, even though they should be accumulated and multiplied a thousandfold. A reassuring
thought for those who may not have many of
these within their reach, a warning thought for
those who might be tempted to put their trust in
them. On the occasion of that Exhibition to
which I have referred, it was well said, 'On the
structure of language are impressed the most distinct and durable records of the habitual operations of the human powers. In the full possession
of language each man has a vast, almost an inex-
haustible, treasure of examples of the most subtle
and varied processes of human thought. Much
apparatus, many material helps, some of them
costly, may be employed to assist education; but
there is no apparatus which is so necessary, or
which can do so much as that which is the most
common and the cheapest—which is always at
hand, and ready for every need. Every language
contains in it the result of a greater number of
educational processes and educational experiments,
than we could by any amount of labour and ingenuity accumulate in any educational exhibition
expressly contrived for such a purpose.'

Being entirely convinced that this is nothing more than the truth, I shall endeavour in my closing lecture to suggest some ways in which you may more effectually use this marvellous implement which you possess to the better fulfilling of that which you have chosen as the task and business of your life. You will gladly hear something upon this matter; for you will never, I trust, disconnect what you may yourselves be learning from the hope and prospect of being enabled thereby to teach others more effectually. If you do, and your studies in this way become a selfish thing, of this you may be sure, that in the end they will prove as barren of profit to yourselves as you are content to leave them barren of profit to others. In one noble line Chaucer has characterized the true scholar:—

> 'And gladly would he learn, and gladly teach.'

Resolve that in the spirit of this line you will work and live.

But take here a word or two of warning before we advance any further. You cannot, of course, expect to make for yourselves any original investigations in language; but you can follow safe guides, such as shall lead you by right paths, even as you may follow such as can only lead you astray. Do not fail to keep in mind that perhaps in no region of human knowledge are there such a multitude of unsafe leaders as in this; for indeed etymology, or the science of the origin of words, is one which many, professing for it an earnest devotion, have done their best or their worst to bring into discredit, and to make the laughing-stock at once of the foolish and the wise. Niebuhr has somewhere noted 'the unspeakable spirit of absurdity' which seemed to possess the ancients, whenever they meddled with this subject; but the charge reaches others beside them. Their mantle, in these later times, has often fallen upon no unworthy successors.

What is commoner, even now, than to find the investigator of words and their origin looking round about him here and there, in all the languages, ancient and modern, to which he has any access, till he lights on some word, it matters little to him in which of these, more or less resembling that which he wishes to derive? and this found, to consider his problem solved, and that in this phantom hunt he has successfully run down his prey. Even Dr. Johnson, with his robust, strong, English common-sense, too often offends in this way. In many respects his Dictionary will probably never be surpassed. We shall never have more concise, more accurate, more vigorous explanations of the present meanings of words than he has furnished. But even those who recognize the most fully this merit in his Dictionary, must allow that he was ill equipped by any previous studies for tracing the past history of words; that in this he errs often and signally; and where the smallest possible amount of knowledge would have preserved him from error; as for instance when he derives the name of the peacock from the peak, or tuft of pointed feathers, on its head! while other derivations proposed by him and others are so far more absurd than this, that when Swift, in ridicule of the whole band of philologers, suggests that 'ostler' is only a contraction of oat-stealer, and 'breeches' of bear-riches, it can scarcely be said that these etymologies are more ridiculous than many which have in sober earnest, and by men of no inconsiderable reputation, been proposed.

Oftentimes in this scheme of random etymology, a word in one language is derived from one in another, in bold defiance of the fact that no points of historic contact or connexion, mediate or immediate, have ever existed between the two; the etymologist not caring to ask himself whether it was thus so much as possible that the word should have passed from the one language to the other; whether in fact the resemblance is not merely superficial and illusory, one which so soon as they are stripped of their accidents, disappear altogether. Take a few specimens of this manner of dealing with words; and first from the earlier etymologists. They are often hopelessly astray, blind leaders of the blind.* Thus, what profit

---

* Ménage is one of these 'blind leaders of the blind,' of whom I have spoken above. With all their real erudition, his two folio volumes, one on French, the other on Italian etymologies, have done nothing but harm to the cause which they professed to further. Génin (*Recréations Philologiques*, p. 12–15) passes a severe but just judgment upon him. I extract from this a sentence or two:—Ménage, comme tous ses dévanciers et la plupart de ses successeurs, semble n'avoir été dirigé que par un seul principe en fait d'étymologie. . . . Le voici dans son expression la

can there come of deducing, as does Varro, 'pavo' from 'pavor,' because of the fear which the harsh shriek of the peacock awakens; or with Pliny, 'panthera' from πανθηριον, because the properties of all beasts meet in the panther; or what can they help who tell us that 'formica,' the ant, is 'ferens micas,' the grain-bearer? Medieval suggestions abound, as vain, and if possible, vainer still. 'Apis,' a bee, is ἄπους or without feet, bees being born without feet, the etymology and the natural history keeping excellent company together. Or what shall we say of deriving 'mors' from 'amarus,' because death is bitter; or from 'Mars,' because death is frequent in war; or 'à *morsu* vetiti pomi,' because that forbidden bite brought death into the world; or with a modern investigator of language, and one of high reputation in his time, deducing 'girl' from 'garrula,' because girls are commonly talkative?

All experience, indeed, proves how perilous it is to etymologize at random, and on the strength of mere surface similarities of sound. Let me

---

plus nette. Tout mot vient du mot qui lui ressemble le mieux. Cela posé, Ménage, avec son érudition polyglotte, s'abat sur le grec, le latin, l'italien, l'espagnol, l'allemand, le celtique, et ne fait difficulté d'aller jusqu'à l'hébreu. C'est dommage que de son tems on ne cultivât pas encore le sanscrit, l'hindoustani, le thibétain et l'arabe; il les eut contraints à lui livrer des étymologies françaises..... Il ne se met pas en peine des chemins par où un mot hébreu ou carthaginois aurait pu passer pour venir s'établir en France. Il y est, le voilà, suffit! L'identité ne peut être mise en question devant la ressemblance. et souvent Dieu sait quelle ressemblance!

illustrate the absurdities into which this may easily betray us by an amusing example. A clergyman, who himself told me the story, had sought, and not unsuccessfully, to kindle in his schoolmaster a passion for the study of derivations. His scholar enquired of him one day if he were aware of the derivation of 'crypt'? He naturally replied in the affirmative, that 'crypt' came from a Greek word to conceal, and meant a covered place, itself concealed, and where things intended to be concealed were placed. The other rejoined that he was quite aware the word was commonly so explained, but he had no doubt erroneously; that 'crypt,' as he had now convinced himself, was in fact contracted from 'cry-pit;' being the pit where in days of Popish tyranny those who were condemned to cruel penances were plunged, and out of which their cry was heard to come up—therefore called the 'cry-pit,' now contracted into 'crypt!' Let me say, before quitting my tale, that I would far sooner a schoolmaster made a hundred such mistakes than that he should be careless and incurious in all which concerned the words which he was using. To make mistakes, as we are on the way to knowledge, is far more honourable than to escape making them through never having set out to seek knowledge.

But while errors like his may very well be pardoned, of this we may be sure, that they will do little in etymology, will continually err and cause others to err, who in these studies leave this out of sight for an instant—namely, that no

amount of resemblance between words in different
languages is of itself sufficient to prove that they
are akin, even as no amount of apparent unlikeness in sound or present form is sufficient to dis-
prove consanguinity. 'Judge not according to
appearance,' must everywhere here be the rule.
One who in many regions of human knowledge
anticipated the discoveries of later times, said well
a century and a half ago, 'Many etymologies are
true, which at the first blush are not probable;' *
and, as he might have added, many appear probable, which are not true. This being so, it is
our wisdom on the one side to distrust superficial
likenesses, on the other not to be dismayed by
superficial differences. I cannot go into this
matter; only I will say, Have no faith in those
which etymologize on the strength of *sounds*, and
not on that of *letters*, and of letters, moreover,
dealt with according to fixed and recognized laws
of equivalence and permutation. Never forget
that illustrious scholar's word, that much in this
region of knowledge is true which does not seem
probable; nor the converse, perhaps still more
important, that much seems probable which is not
true. For an example of this last, 'Auge,' the
German form of our 'eye,' is in every letter
identical with the Greek for splendour $(α\dot{υ}γή)$;
and yet, though there is a very intimate connexion between German and Greek, these have no

---

* Leibnitz (*Opp.* vol. v. p. 61): Sæpe fit ut etymologiæ veræ
sint, quæ primo aspectu verisimiles non sunt.

relation with one another whatever; while, on the other hand, little, or almost nothing, as there seems of contact between 'Auge' and 'oculus,' they are certainly the same word. Who, again, would not take for granted that our 'much' and the Spanish 'mucho,' identical in meaning, were also in etymology nearly related? There is no connexion between them. Not many years ago a considerable scholar identified the Greek 'holos' (ὅλος) and our 'whole.' Many, if I mistake not, have been tempted to do the same. There is as little connexion between these.

Here then, as elsewhere, the condition of all successful investigation is to have learned to despise phenomena, the deceitful shows and appearances of things; to have resolved to reach and to grapple with the things themselves. It is the fable of Proteus over again. He will take a thousand shapes wherewith he will seek to elude and delude one who is determined to obtain from him that true answer, which he is capable of yielding, but will only yield on compulsion. The true investigator is deceived by none of these. He still holds him fast; binds him in strong chains; until he takes his own and his true shape at the last; and answers as a true seer, whatever question may be put to him. Nor, let me say by the way, will that man's gain be small who, having learned to distrust the obvious and the plausible, carries into other regions of study and of action the lessons which he has thus learned; determines to seek the ground of things, and to plant his foot upon that; to believe that a lie may look very fair, and yet be a lie after all; that the truth may show very unattractive, very unlike and paradoxical, and yet be the very truth notwithstanding.

To return from a long, but not needless digression. Convinced as I am of the immense advantage of following up words to their sources, of 'deriving' them, that is, of tracing each little rill to the river whence it was first drawn, I can conceive no method of so effectually defacing and barbarizing our English tongue, of practically emptying it of all the hoarded wit, wisdom, imagination, and history which it contains, of cutting the vital nerve which connects its present with the past, as the introduction of the scheme of phonetic spelling, which some have lately been zealously advocating among us. I need hardly tell you the principle of this is that all words should be spelt as they are sounded, that the writing should, in every case, be subordinated to the speaking.* This, which is everywhere tacitly assumed, as not needing any proof, is the fallacy which runs through the whole system. There is, indeed, no necessity for this. Every word, on the contrary, has *two* existences, as a spoken word and a written; and you have no right to sacrifice one of

---

* I do not know whether the advocates of phonetic spelling have urged the authority and practice of Augustus as being in their favour. Suetonius, among other amusing gossip about this Emperor, records of him: Videtur eorum sequi opinionem, qui perinde scribendum ac loquamur, existiment (*Octavius*, c. 88).

these, or even to subordinate it wholly, to the other. A word exists as truly for the eye as for the ear; and in a highly advanced state of society, where reading is almost as universal as speaking, quite as much for the one as for the other. That in the *written* word moreover is the permanence and continuity of language and of learning, and that the connexion is most intimate of a true orthography with all this, is affirmed in our words, 'letters,' 'literature,' 'unlettered,' as in other languages by words exactly corresponding to these.*

The gains consequent on the introduction of such a change would be insignificantly small, the losses enormously great. There would be gain in the saving of a certain amount of the labour now spent in learning to spell; an amount of labour, however, absurdly exaggerated by the promoters of the scheme. But even this gain would not long remain, seeing that pronunciation is itself continually altering; custom is lord here for better and for worse; and a multitude of words are now pronounced in a manner different from that of a hundred years ago, indeed from that of ten years ago; so that, before very long, there would again be a chasm between the spelling and the pronunciation of words;—unless indeed the spelling varied, which it could not consistently refuse to do, as the pronunciation varied, reproducing each of its capricious or barbarous alterations; these

---

* As γράμματα, ἀγράμματος, *litteræ*, *belles-lettres*.

last, it must be remembered, being changes not in the pronunciation only, but in the word itself, which would only exist as pronounced, the written word being a mere shadow servilely waiting upon the spoken. When these changes had multiplied a little, and they would indeed multiply exceedingly, so soon as the barrier which now exists was removed, what the language would before long become, it is not easy to guess.

This fact, however, though sufficient to show how ineffectual the scheme of phonetic spelling would prove, even for the removing of those inconveniences which it proposes to remedy, is only the smallest objection to it. The far more serious objection is, that in words out of number it would obliterate those clear marks of birth and parentage, which they bear now upon their fronts, or are ready, upon a very slight interrogation, to reveal. Words have now an ancestry; and the ancestry of words, as of men, is often a very noble part of them, making them capable of great things, because those from whom they are descended have done great things before them; but this would deface their scutcheon, and bring them all to the same ignoble level. Words are now a nation, grouped into tribes and families, some smaller, some larger; this change would go far to reduce them to a promiscuous and barbarous horde. Now they are often translucent with their inner thought, lighted up by it; in how many cases would this inner light be then quenched? They have now a body and a soul, the soul quickening the body; then oftentimes nothing but a body, forsaken by the spirit of life, would remain. Both these objections were urged long ago by Bacon, who characterizes this so-called reformation, 'that writing should be consonant to speaking,' as 'a branch of unprofitable subtlety;' and especially urges that thereby 'the derivations of words, especially from foreign languages, are utterly defaced and extinguished.'

From the results of various approximations to phonetic spelling, which at different times have been made, and the losses thereon ensuing, we may guess what the loss would be were the system fully carried out. Of those fairly acquainted with Latin, it would be curious to know how many have seen 'silva' in 'savage,' since it has been so written, and not 'salvage,' as of old? or have been reminded of the hindrances to a civilized and human society which the indomitable forest, more perhaps than any other obstacle, presents. When 'fancy' was spelt 'phant'sy,' as by Sylvester in his translation of Du Bartas, and other scholarly writers of the seventeenth century, no one could doubt of its identity with 'phantasy,' as no Greek scholar could miss its relation with φαντασία. Spell 'analyse' as I have sometimes seen it, and as phonetically it ought to be, 'analize,' and the tap-root of the word is cut. What number of readers will recognize in it then the image of dissolving and resolving aught into its elements, and use it with a more or less conscious reference to this? It may be urged that few do so even now.

The more need they should not be fewer; for these few do in fact retain the word in its place, from which else it might gradually drift; they preserve its vitality, and the propriety of its use, not merely for themselves, but also for the others that have not this knowledge. In phonetic spelling is, in brief, the proposal that the learned and the educated should of free choice place themselves under the disadvantages of the ignorant and uneducated, instead of seeking to elevate these last to their own more favoured condition. *

Even now the relationships of words, so important for our right understanding of them, are continually overlooked; a very little matter serving to conceal from us the family to which they pertain. Thus how many of our nouns are indeed unsuspected participles, or are otherwise most

---

* The same attempt to introduce phonography has been several times made, once in the sixteenth century, and again some thirty years ago, in France. What would be there the results? We may judge of these from the results of a partial application of the system. 'Temps' is now written 'tems,' the *p* having been ejected as superfluous. What is the consequence? at once its visible connexion with the Latin 'tempus,' with the Spanish 'tiempo,' with the Italian 'tempo,' with its own 'temporel' and 'temporaire,' is broken, and for many effaced. Or note the results from another point of view. Here are 'poids' a weight, 'poix' pitch, 'pois' peas. No one could mark in speaking the distinction between these; and thus to the ear there may be confusion between them, but to the eye there is none; not to say that the *d* in 'poids' puts it for us in relation with 'pondus,' the *x* in 'poix' with 'pix,' the *s* in 'pois' with the low Latin 'pisum.' In each case the letter which these reformers would dismiss as useless, and worse than useless, keeps the secret of the word.

closely connected with verbs, with which we probably never think of putting them in relation. And yet with how lively an interest shall we discover those to be of closest kin, which we had never considered but as entire strangers to one another; what increased mastery over our mother tongue shall we through such discoveries obtain. Thus the 'smith' has his name from the sturdy blows that he 'smites' upon the anvil; 'wrong' is the perfect participle of 'to wring,' that which has been 'wrung' or wrested from the right; as in French 'tort,' from 'torqueo,' is the twisted; the 'brunt' of the battle is its heat, where it 'burns' the most fiercely; the 'haft' of a knife, that whereby you 'have' or hold it.

This exercise of putting words in their true relation and connexion with one another might be carried much further. Of whole groups of words, which may seem to acknowledge no kinship with one another, it will not be difficult to show that they had a common parentage and descent. For instance, here are 'shire,' 'shore,' 'share,' 'shears;' 'shred,' 'sherd;' all derived from one Anglo-Saxon word, which signifies to separate or divide, and still exists with us in the shape of 'to sheer,' which made once the three perfects, 'shore,' 'share,' 'shered.' 'Shire' is a district in England, separated from the rest; a 'share' is a portion of anything thus divided off; 'shears' are instruments effecting this process of separation; the 'shore' is the place where the continuity of the land is interrupted or separated by the sea; a 'shred' is that which is 'shered' or shorn from the main piece; a 'sherd,' as a pot-'sherd,' (also 'pot-share,' Spenser,) that which is broken off and thus divided from the vessel; these not at all exhausting this group or family of words, though it would take more time than we can spare to put some other words in their relation with it.

But this analysing of groups of words for the detecting of the bond of relationship between them, and their common root, may require more etymological knowledge than you possess, and more helps from books than you can always command. There is another process, and one which may prove no less useful to yourselves and to others, which will lie more certainly within your reach. You will meet in books, sometimes in the same book, and perhaps in the same page of this book, a word used in senses so far apart from one another, that at first it will seem to you absurd to suppose any bond of connexion between them. Now when you thus fall in with a word employed in these two or more senses so far removed from one another, accustom yourselves to seek out the bond which there certainly is between these several uses. This tracing of that which is common to and connects all its meanings can only be done by getting to its centre and heart, to the seminal meaning, from which, as from a fruitful seed, all the others unfold themselves; to the first link in the chain, from which every later one, in a direct line or a lateral, depends. We may proceed in this investigation, certain that we shall find such, or at least that such there is to be found. For nothing can be more certain than this (and the non-recognition of it is a serious blemish in Johnson's *Dictionary*), that a word has originally but one meaning, that all other uses, however widely they may diverge from one another and recede from this one, may yet be affiliated upon it, brought back to the one central meaning, which grasps and knits them all together; just as the races of men, black, white, and red, despite of all their present diversity and dispersion, have a central point of unity in that one pair from which they all have descended.

Let me illustrate this by two or three familiar examples. How various are the senses in which 'post' is used; as 'post'-office; 'post'-haste; a 'post' standing in the ground; a military 'post;' an official 'post;' 'to post' a ledger. Is it possible to find anything which is common to all these uses of 'post'? When once we are on the right track, nothing is easier. 'Post' is the Latin 'positus,' that which is *placed*; the piece of timber is 'placed' in the ground, and so a 'post;' a military station is a 'post,' for a man is 'placed' in it, and must not quit it without orders; to travel 'post,' is to have certain relays of horses 'placed' at intervals, that so no delay on the road may occur; the 'post'-office avails itself of this mode of communication; to 'post' a ledger is to 'place' or register its several items.

Once more, in what an almost infinite number

of senses 'stock' is employed; we have live
'stock,' 'stock' in trade, the village 'stocks,' the
'stock' of a gun, the 'stock'-dove, the 'stocks'
on which ships are built, the 'stock' which goes
round the neck, the family 'stock,' the 'stocks,'
or public funds, in which money is invested, with
other 'stocks' besides these. What point in common
can we find between them all? This, that
being all derived from the verb 'to stick,' they
cohere in the idea of *fixedness*, which is common
to them all. Thus, the 'stock' of a gun is that
in which the barrel is fixed; the village 'stocks'
are those in which the feet are fastened; the
'stock' in trade is the fixed capital; and so too,
the 'stock' on the farm, although the fixed capital
has there taken the shape of horses and cattle; in
the 'stocks' or public funds, money sticks fast,
inasmuch as those who place it there cannot withdraw
or demand the capital, but receive only the
interest; the 'stock' of a tree is fast set in the
ground; and from this use of the word it is transferred
to a family; the 'stock' or 'stirps' is that
from which it grows, and out of which it unfolds
itself. And here we may bring in the 'stock'-dove,
as being the 'stock' or 'stirps' of the
domestic kinds. I might group with these, 'stake'
in both its spellings; a 'stake' is stuck in the
hedge and there remains; the 'stakes' which men
wager against the issue of a race are paid down,
and thus fixed or deposited to answer the event;
a beef-'steak' is a portion so small that it can be
stuck on the point of a fork; and so forward.

How often does the 'quick' of the Creed perplex children. They learn indeed that 'the quick' there are the living; yet know it only on trust; for they fail to connect this 'quick' with the 'quick' of their own vocabulary, the 'quick' with which one bids another to throw up the ball, or the 'quick'-set hedge which runs round their father's garden, or the 'quick' parts for which some unwise visitor has praised one of them at school, with the 'quick'-silver of the barometer, or the 'quick'-sands which they read of in their manuals of geography. Yet that all these are the same 'quick,' it would be at once easy and instructive to show them.

When we thus affirm that the divergent meanings of a word can all be brought back to some one point from which, immediately or mediately, they every one proceed, that none has primarily more than one meaning, it must be remembered that there may very well be two words, or it may be more, spelt as well as pronounced alike, which yet are wholly different in their derivation and primary usage; and that, of course, between such homonyms as these no bond of union on the score of this identity is to be sought. Neither does this fact in the least invalidate the assertion. We have in such cases, as Cobbett has expressed it well, the same combination of letters, but not the same word. Thus we have 'page,' the side of a leaf, from 'pagina,' and 'page,' a small boy, the Greek 'paidion;' 'league,' a treaty, from 'ligare,' to bind, and 'league' (leuca), a measure of distance, a word of Celtic origin; 'host' (hostis), an army, and 'host' (hostia), in the Roman Catholic sacrifice of the mass; 'riddle,' a sieve or small network, the Latin 'reticulum,' and 'riddle,' an enigma, from another source; the 'Mosaic' law, or law of Moses, and 'mosaic' work ('opus *musivum*'), work graceful, as connected with the *Muses*. We have two 'ounces' (uncia and onze); two 'seals' (sigillum and scol); two 'lakes' (lacus and lacca); two 'kennels' (canalis and canile); two 'schools,' a 'school' of philosophy, a 'school' of whales (schola and sceol); two 'partisans' (partisan and partesana); two 'quires' (choir and cahier) two verbs 'to allow' (allocare and allaudare); three 'rapes,' (as the 'rape' of Proserpine, the 'rape' of Bramber, 'rape'-seed); four 'ports' (porta, portus, port, Oporto); while other duplicate or more than duplicate words in the language are the following: 'toil,' 'shrub,' 'plot,' 'bull,' 'mole,' 'crowd,' 'gulf,' 'dole,' 'date,' 'mint,' 'punch,' 'plot,' 'ear,' 'gust,' 'pulse,' 'pernicious.' You will find it profitable to follow these up at home, to trace out the two or more words which have clothed themselves in exactly the same outward form, and on what etymologies they severally repose; so too, as often as you suspect the existence of homonyms, to make proof of the matter for yourselves, gradually forming as complete a list of these as you can. You may usefully do the same in any other language which you study, for they exist in all. In all these the identity is merely on the surface and in sound, and it would, of course, be lost labour to seek for a point of contact between meanings which have no closer connexion with one another in reality than they have in appearance.

Let me suggest some further exercises in this region of words. There are some which at once provoke and promise to reward inquiry, by the evident readiness with which they will yield up the secret, if duly interrogated by us. Many, as we have seen, have defied, and will probably defy to the end, all efforts to dissipate the mystery which hangs over them; and these we must be content to leave; but many announce that their explanations cannot be very far to seek. Let me instance 'candidate.' Does it not argue an incurious spirit to be content that this word should be given and received by us a hundred times, as at a contested election it is, and we never to ask ourselves, What does it mean? why is one offering himself to the choice of his fellows, called a 'candidate'? If the word lay evidently beyond our horizon, we might acquiesce in our ignorance; but resting, as manifestly it does, upon the Latin 'candidus,' it challenges inquiry, and a very little of this would at once put us in possession of the Roman custom for which it witnesses—namely, that such as intended to claim the suffrages of the people for any of the chief offices of the State, presented themselves beforehand to them in a *white* toga, being therefore called 'candidati.' And as it so often happens that in seeking information on one subject we obtain it upon another, so will it probably be here; for in fully learning

what this custom was, you will hardly fail to
learn how we obtained 'ambition,' what originally
it meant, and how Milton should have written—

'To reign is worth ambition, though in hell.'

Or again, any one who knows so much as that
'verbum' means a word, might well be struck by
the fact (and if he followed it up would be led far
into the relation of the parts of speech to one
another), that in grammar it is not employed to
signify any word whatsoever, but restricted to
the verb alone; 'verbum' is the verb. Surely
here is matter for reflection. What gives to the
verb the right to monopolize the dignity of being
'the word'? Is it because the verb is the animating power, the vital principle of every sentence,
and that without which, understood or uttered, no
sentence can exist? or can you offer any other
reason? I leave this to your own consideration.

We call certain books 'classics.' We have indeed a double use of the word, for we speak of
Greek and Latin as the 'classical' languages, and
the great writers in these as *the* classics;' while
at other times you hear of a 'classical' English
style, or of English 'classics.' Now 'classic' is
connected plainly with 'classis.' What then does
it mean in itself, and how has it arrived at this
double use? 'The term is drawn from the political economy of Rome. Such a man was rated
as to his income in the third class, such another in
the fourth, and so on; but he who was in the
highest was emphatically said to be of *the* class,

"classicus"—a class man, without adding the number, as in that case superfluous; while all others were infra classem. Hence, by an obvious analogy, the best authors were rated as "classici," or men of the highest class; just as in English we say "men of rank" absolutely, for men who are in the highest ranks of the state.' The mental process by which this title, which would apply rightly to the best authors in *all* languages, came to be restricted to those only in two, and these two to be claimed, to the seeming exclusion of all others, as *the* classical languages, is one constantly recurring, making itself felt in all regions of human thought; to which therefore I would in passing call your attention, though I cannot now do more.

There is one circumstance which you must by no means suffer to escape your own notice, nor that of your pupils—namely, that words out of number, which are now employed only in a figurative sense, did yet originally rest on some fact of the outward world, vividly presenting itself to the imagination; which fact the word has incorporated and knit up with itself for ever. If I may judge from my own experience, few intelligent boys would not feel that they had gotten something, when made to understand that 'to insult' means properly to leap as on the prostrate body of a foe; 'to affront,' to strike him on the face; that 'to succour' means by running to place oneself under one that is falling; 'to relent,' (connected with 'lentus,' not 'lenis,') to slacken the swiftness of one's pursuit;* 'to reprehend,' to lay hold of one with the intention of forcibly pulling him back; 'to exonerate,' to discharge of a burden, as when a ship is unladen; that 'to be examined' means to be weighed. They would be pleased to learn that a man is called 'supercilious,' because haughtiness with contempt of others expresses itself by the raising of the eyebrows or 'supercilium;' that 'subtle' (subtilis for subtexilis) is literally 'fine-spun;' that 'astonished' (attonitus) is properly thunderstruck; that 'imbecile,' which we use for weak, and now always for weak in intellect, means strictly (unless indeed we must renounce this etymology), leaning upon a staff (in bacillo), as one aged or infirm might do; that 'chaste' is properly white, 'castus' being a participle of 'candeo,' as is now generally allowed; that 'sincere' may be, I dare not say that it is, without wax, (sine cerâ,) as the best and finest honey should be; that a 'companion,' probably at least, is one with whom we share our bread, a messmate; that a 'sarcasm' is properly such a lash inflicted by 'the scourge of the tongue' as brings away the *flesh* after it; with much more in the same kind.

'Trivial' is a word borrowed from the life. Mark three or four persons standing idly at the point where one street bisects at right angles another, and discussing there the idle nothings of the day; there you have the living explanation of

---

* 'But nothing might *relent* his hasty flight.' Spenser.

'trivial,' 'trivialities,' such as no explanation not rooting itself in the etymology would ever give you, or enable you to give to others. You have there the 'tres viæ,' the 'trivium;' and 'trivialities' properly mean such talk as is holden by those idle loiterers that gather at this meeting of three roads.* 'Rivals' properly are those who dwell on the banks of the same river. But as all experience shows, there is no such fruitful source of contention as a water-right, and these would be often at strife with one another in regard of the periods during which they severally had a right to the use of the stream, turning it off into their own fields before the time, or leaving open the sluices beyond the time, or in other ways interfering, or being counted to interfere, with the rights of their neighbours. And in this way 'rivals' came to be applied to any who were on any grounds in unfriendly competition with one another.

By such teaching as this you may often improve, and that without turning play-time into lesson-time, the hours of relaxation and amusement. But 'relaxation,' on which we have just lighted as by chance, must not escape us. How can the bow be 'relaxed' or slackened (for this

---

* I have allowed this explanation to stand; yet with many misgivings whether 'trivial' is not from 'trivium' in another sense; that is, from the 'trivium,' or three preparatory disciplines, —grammar, arithmetic, and geometry,—as contrasted with the four more advanced, or 'quadrivium,' which together were esteemed in the Middle Ages to constitute a complete liberal education. Preparatory schools were called often '*trivial* schools,' as occupying themselves with the 'trivium.'

is the image), which has not been bent, whose string has never been drawn tight? Having drawn tight the bow of our mind by earnest toil, we may then claim to have it from time to time 'relaxed.' Having been attentive and assiduous, then, but not otherwise, we may claim 'relaxation' and amusement. But 'attentive' and 'assiduous' are themselves words which will repay us to understand exactly what they mean. He is 'assiduous,' who sits close to his work; he is 'attentive,' who, being taught, stretches out his neck that so he may not lose a word. 'Diligence' too has its lesson. Derived from 'diligo,' to love, it reminds us that the secret of true industry in our work is love of that work. And as truth is wrapped up in 'diligence,' what a lie, on the other hand, lurks at the root of 'indolence,' or, to speak more accurately, of our present employment of it! This, from 'in' and 'doleo,' not to grieve, is properly a state in which we have no grief or pain; and employed as we now employ it, would have us to believe that indulgence in sloth constitutes for us the truest negation of pain. Now no one would wish to deny that 'pain' and 'pains' are often nearly allied; but yet these pains hand us over to true pleasures; while indolence is so far from yielding that good which it is so forward to promise, that Cowper spoke only truth, when, perhaps meaning to witness against a falsehood here, he spoke of

'Lives spent in *indolence*, and therefore *sad*,'

not 'therefore *glad*,' as the word 'indolence' would fain have us to believe.

There is another way in which these studies I have been urging may be turned to account. Doubtless you will seek to cherish in your scholars, to keep lively in yourselves, that spirit and temper which find a special interest in all relating to the land of our birth, that land which the providence of God has assigned as the sphere of our life's task and of theirs. Our schools are called 'national,' and if we would have them such in reality, we must neglect nothing that will foster a national spirit in them. I know not whether this is sufficiently considered among us; yet certainly we cannot have Church schools worthy the name, least of all in England, unless they are truly national as well. It is the anti-national character of the Romish system, though I do not in the least separate this from the anti-scriptural, but rather regard the two as most intimately connected, which mainly revolts Englishmen; and if their sense of this should ever grow weak, their protest against that system would soon lose much of its energy and strength. Now here, as everywhere else, knowledge must be the food of love. Your pupils must know something about England, if they are to love it; they must see some connexion of its past with its present, of what it has been with what it is, if they are to feel that past as anything to them.

And as no impresses of the past are so abiding, so none, when once attention has been awakened to them, are so self-evident as those which names preserve; although, without this calling of the

attention to them, the most broad and obvious of
these foot-prints of time may continue to escape
our observation to the end of our lives. Leibnitz
tells us, and one can quite understand, the delight
with which a great German Emperor, Maximilian
the First, discovered that 'Habsburg,' or 'Hapsburg,' the ancestral name of his house, really had
a meaning, one moreover full of vigour and poetry.
This he did, when he heard it by accident on the
lips of a Swiss peasant, no longer cut short and
thus disguised, but in its original fulness,
'Habichtsburg,' or 'Hawk's-Tower,' being no
doubt the name of the castle which was the cradle
of his race. Of all the thousands of Englishmen
who are aware that the Angles and Saxons established themselves in this island, and that we are
in the main descended from them, it would be
curious to know how many have realized to themselves a fact so obvious as that this 'England'
means 'Angle-land,' or that in the names 'Essex,'
'Sussex,' and 'Middlesex,' we preserve a record
of East Saxons, South Saxons, and Middle Saxons,
who occupied those several portions of the land;
or that 'Norfolk' and 'Suffolk' are two broad
divisions of 'northern' and 'southern folk,' into
which the East Anglian kingdom was divided.
'Cornwall' does not bear its origin quite so plainly
upon its front, or tell its story so that everyone
who runs may read. At the same time its secret
is not hard to attain to. As the Teutonic immigrants advanced, such of the British population as
was not absorbed by them retreated, as we all

have learned, into Wales and Cornwall, that is, till they could retreat no further. This fact is evidently preserved in the name of 'Wales,' which means properly The foreigners,—the nations of Teutonic blood calling all bordering tribes by this name. But though not quite so apparent on the surface, this fact is also preserved in 'Cornwall,' written formerly 'Cornwales,' or the land inhabited by the Welsh of the Corn or Horn. The chroniclers uniformly speak of North Wales and Corn-Wales.* These Angles, Saxons, and Britons or Welshmen, about whom our pupils may be reading, will be to them more like actual men of flesh and blood, who indeed trod this same soil which we are treading now, when we can, thus point to traces surviving to the present day, which they have left behind them, and which England, as long as it is England, will retain.

The Danes too have left their marks on the land. We all probably are, more or less, aware how much Danish blood runs in English veins; what large colonies from Scandinavia (for probably as many came from Norway as from modern Denmark) settled in some parts of this island. It will be interesting to show that the limits of this Danish settlement and occupation may even now be confidently traced by the constant recurrence in all such districts of the names of towns and villages ending in 'bye,' which signified in their language, a dwelling or single village; as

---

* Isaac Taylor, *Names and Places*, 2nd edit., p. 63.

Netherby, Appleby, Derby, Whitby. Thus if you examine closely a map of Lincolnshire, one of the chief seats of Danish immigration, you will find one hundred, or well nigh a fourth part, of the towns and villages to have this ending, the whole coast being studded with them; while here in Hampshire it is utterly unknown. Or, again draw a line transversely through England from Canterbury by London to Chester, the line, that is, of the great Roman road, called Watling Street, and north of this six hundred instances of its occurrence may be found, while to the south there are almost none. 'Thorpe,' equivalent to the German 'dorf,' as Bishopsthorpe, Althorp, tells the same tale of a Norse occupation of the soil; and the termination, somewhat rarer, of 'thwaite' no less. On the other hand, where, as in this south of England, the ' hams' abound (the word is identical with our ' home '), as Buckingham, Egham, Shoreham, there you may be sure that not Norsemen but Germans proper took possession of the soil. ' Worth ' or ' worthy,' signifying, as it does, the place warded or guarded, tells the same story, as Bosworth, Kingsworthy. The 'stokes' in like manner, as Basingstoke, Itchenstoke, are Saxon, being places stockaded, with stocks or piles for defence.

You are yourselves learning, or hereafter you may be teaching others, the names and number of the English counties or shires. What a dull routine task for them and for you this may be, supplying no food for the intellect, no points of

attachment for any of its higher powers to take
hold of! And yet in these two little words, 'shire'
and 'county,' if you would make them render up
even a small part of their treasure, what lessons
of English history are contained! One who knows
the origin of these names, and how we come to
possess such a double nomenclature, looks far into
the social condition of England in that period
when the strong foundations of all that has since
made England glorious and great were being laid;
by aid of these words may detect links which
bind its present to its remotest past; for of lands
as of persons it may be said, 'the child is father
of the man.' 'Shire,' as I observed just now, is
connected with 'shear,' 'share,' and is properly
a portion 'shered' or 'shorn' off. When a Saxon
king would create an earl, it did not lie in men's
thoughts, accustomed as they were to deal with
realities, that such could be a merely titular creation, or exist without territorial jurisdiction; and
a 'share' or 'shire' was assigned him to govern,
which also gave him his title. But at the Conquest this Saxon officer was displaced by a Norman,
the 'earl' by the 'count'—this title of 'count'
borrowed from the later Roman empire, meaning
originally 'companion' (comes), one who had the
honour of being closest companion to his leader;
and the 'shire' was now the 'county' (comitatus),
as governed by this 'comes.' In that singular and
inexplicable fortune of words, which causes some
to disappear and die out under the circumstances
apparently most favourable for life, others to hold

their ground when all seemed against them,
'count' has disappeared from the titles of English
nobility, while 'earl' has recovered its place;
although in evidence of the essential identity of
the two titles, or offices rather, the wife of the
earl is entitled a 'countess;' and in further
memorial of these great changes that so long ago
came over our land, the two names 'shire' and
'county' equally survive as in the main interchangeable words in our mouths.

A great part of England, all that portion of it
which the Saxons occupied, is divided into 'hundreds.' Have you ever asked yourselves what this
division means, for something it must mean?
The 'hundred' is supposed to have been originally
a group or settlement of one hundred free families
of Saxon colonists. If this was so, we have at once
an explanation of the immense disproportion between the area of the 'hundred' in the southern
and in the more northern counties—the average
number of square miles in a 'hundred' of Sussex
or Kent being three or four and twenty; of Lancashire more than three hundred. The Saxon population would naturally be far the densest in the
earlier settlements of the east and south, while
more to west and north the Saxon tenure would
be one rather of conquest than of colonization,
and the free families much fewer and more scattered. But further you have noticed, I dare say,
the exceptional fact that the county of Sussex,
besides the division into hundreds, is divided also
into 'rapes;' thus the 'rape' of Bramber, and so

on. Now this 'rape' is a memorial of the violent transfer of landed property by William the Conqueror, the lands being rudely plotted out for division by the 'rope' or 'rape,' which was a favourite way with these Norman intruders; and thus we keep in this word a memento to the present day in our language of the rough and ready processes adopted by the men of other times.*

Let us a little consider, in conclusion, how we may usefully bring our etymologies and other notices of words to bear on the religious teaching which we would impart in our schools. To do this with much profit we must often deal with words as the Queen does with the gold and silver coin of the realm. When this has been current long, and by often passing from man to man, with perhaps occasional clipping in dishonest hands, has lost not only the clear brightness, the well-defined sharpness of outline, but much of the weight and intrinsic value which it had when first issued from the royal mint, it is the sovereign's prerogative to recall it, and issue it anew, with the royal image stamped on it afresh, bright and sharp, weighty and full, as at first. Now to a process such as this the true mint-masters of language, and all of us may be such, will often submit the words which they use. Where use and custom have worn away their significance, we too may recall and issue them afresh. With how many

---

* Isaac Taylor, *Names and Places*, 2nd edit. pp. 192, 365.

it has thus fared!—for example, with one which will be often in your mouths. You speak of the 'lessons' of the day; but what is 'lessons' here for most of us save a lazy synonym for the morning and evening chapters appointed to be read in church? But realize what the Church intended in calling these chapters by this name; namely, that they should be the daily instruction of her children; listen to them yourselves as such; lead your scholars to regard them as such, and in this use of 'lessons' what a lesson for every one of us there may be! 'Bible' itself, while we not irreverently use it, may yet be no more to us than the sign by which we designate the written Word of God. Keep in mind that it properly means the book, and nothing more; that once it could be employed of any book (in Chaucer it is so), and what matter of thought and reflection lies in this our present restriction of 'bible' to one book, to the exclusion of all others! So strong has been the sense of Holy Scripture being *the* Book, the worthiest and best, that one which explained all other books, standing up in their midst,—like Joseph's kingly sheaf, to which all the other sheaves did obeisance,—that this name of 'Bible' or 'Book' has been restrained to it alone: just as 'Scripture' means no more than 'writing;' but this inspired Writing has been acknowledged so far above all other writings, that this name also it has obtained as exclusively its own.

Again, something may be learned from knowing

that the 'surname,' as distinguished from the 'Christian' name, is the name over and above, not 'sire'-name, or name received from the father, as some explain, but 'sur'-name (super nomen). There was never, that is, a time when every baptized man had not a Christian name, the recognition of his personal standing before God; while the surname, the name expressing his relation, not to the kingdom of God, but to a worldly society, is of much later growth, superadded to the other, as the word itself declares. What a lesson at once in the growing up of a human society, and in the contrast between it and the heavenly Society of the Church, might be appended to this explanation! There was a period when only a few had surnames; had, that is, any significance in the order of things temporal; while the Christian name from the first was common to every man. All this might be brought usefully to bear on your exposition of the first words in the Catechism.

There are long Latin words, which, desire as we may to use all plainness of speech, we cannot do without, nor find their adequate substitutes in other parts of our language; words which must always remain the vehicles of much of that truth by which we live. Now in explaining these, make it your rule always to start, where you can, from the derivation, and to return to that as often as you can. Thus you wish to explain 'revelation.' How much will be gained if you can attach some distinct image to the word, one to which your scholars, as often as they hear it, may mentally recur. Nor is this impossible. God's 'revelation' of Himself is a drawing back of the veil or curtain which concealed Him from men; not man finding out God, but God discovering Himself to man; all which is contained in the word. Or you wish to explain 'absolution.' Many will know that it has something to do with the pardon of sins; but how much more accurately will they know this, when they know that 'to absolve' means 'to loosen from:' God's 'absolution' of men being his releasing of them from the bands of those sins with which they were bound. Here every one will connect a distinct image with the word, such as will always come to his help when he would realize what its precise meaning may be. That which was done for Lazarus naturally, the Lord exclaiming, 'Loose him, and let him go,' the same is done spiritually for us, when we receive the 'absolution' of our sins.

Tell them that 'atonement' means 'at-one-ment'—the setting at one of those who were at twain before, namely God and man, and they will attach to 'atonement' a definite meaning, which perhaps in no way else it would have possessed for them; and from this you may muster the passages in Scripture which describe the sinner's state as one of separation, estrangement, alienation, from God, the Christian's state as one in which he walks together with God, because the two have been set 'at one.' Or you have to deal with the following, 'to redeem,' 'Redeemer,' 'redemption.' Lose not yourselves in vague generalities, but fasten on the central point of these, that they imply a 'buying,' and not this merely, but a 'buying back;' and then connect with them, so explained, the whole circle of Scriptures which rest on this image, which speak of sin as a slavery, of sinners as bondsmen of Satan, of Christ's blood as a ransom, of the Christian as one restored to his liberty.

Many words more suggest themselves; I will not urge more than one; but that one, because in it is a lesson more for ourselves than for others, and with such I would fain bring these lectures to a close. How solemn a truth we express naming our work in this world our 'vocation,' or, which is the same in homelier Anglo-Saxon, our 'calling.' What a calming, elevating, ennobling view of the tasks appointed us in this world, this word gives us. We did not come to our work by accident; we did not choose it for ourselves; but, under much which may wear the appearance of accident and self-choosing, came to it by God's leading and appointment. How will this consideration help us to appreciate justly the dignity of our work, though it were far humbler work, even in the eyes of men, than that of any one of us here present! What an assistance in calming unsettled thoughts and desires, such as would make us wish to be something else than that which we are! What a source of confidence, when we are tempted to lose heart, and to doubt whether we shall carry through our work with any blessing or profit to ourselves or to others! It is our 'vocation,' not out choosing but our 'calling;' and He who 'called' us to it, will, if only we will ask Him, fit us for it, and strengthen us in it.

INDEX OF WORDS.

	PAGE		PAGE
Abbacinare	57	Bantam	123
Absolution	257	Basilisk	45
Acheron	42	Bayonet	122
Allfront	244	Beatitas, beatitudo	157
Agate	122	Bezant	122
Albion	40	Bible	255
Allegiance	203	Biggen	123
Alemanni	138	Bishop	174
Alligator	162	Blackbird	131
Alms	174	Blague, blagueur	109
Ambition	243	Bohemian	124
America	123	Bonhommie	75
Amethyst	131	Book	128
Analyse	234	Door	58
Ananas	101	Brunt	230
Anglia	142	Burke	106
Animosity	80		
Apocryphal	181	Cagot	170
Arras	122	Calamitas	120
Ascendency	130	Calculation	127
Asia Minor	139	Calico	123
Assassin	108	Calling	258
Assentation	68	Cambric	122
Assentator	68	Camelopard	44
Assiduous	247	Canada	177
Astonish	205	Candidate	242
Athanasius	28	Candle	191
Attentive	247	Cannibal	177
Atonement	257	Canonical	134
Avunculize	107	Caprice	30
		Capuchin	110
Baldachin	122	Carbunculus	47

INDEX OF WORDS.

Word	PAGE	Word	PAGE
Cardinal	108	Damson	122
Castus	245	Days of the week	142
Catchpole	90	Delf	122
Catholic	117	Demonetize	153
Caucus	177	Demure	58
Cerfvolant	45	Dénigreur	64
Chaste	245	Derivation	204
Cheat, cheater	90	Desultory	30
Cherry	123	Desynonymize	100, 102
Chevalier d'Industrie	81	Diaper	122
Chrestus	75	Dilapidated	0
Christian	138, 140	Diligence	247
Christology	172	Dimity	122
Christus	75	Dinde	124
Church	102	Dirne	59
Cicerone	80	Disastrous	130
Classical	110	Discernment	210
Classics	243	Discretion	210
Club	91	Distemper	120
Cockatrice	115	Dittany	174
Cocytus	42	Diversion	8
Companion	245	Dominican	28
Conciliatrix	81	Dragonnade	104
Convertisseur	104	Drepanum	40
Convey	60	Druid	125
Cordwain	122	Dunce	110
Cornwall	249		
Cosmopolite	151	Eau de vie	82
Cosmos	140	Ecstasy	205
Count	252	Electrum	180
County	252	Eleemosynary	174
Crafty	68	Elend	51
Crape	122	England	142
Cravat	123	Epiphanes	28
Crypt	228	Episcopal	174
Crystal	114	Ermine	129
Curfew	121	Escheat	90
Currant	123	Euemplastic	157
Cynarctomachy	107	Essay	171
Cyprian	28	Europe	138
		Expend, expense	127, 128
Dactyle	40	Extrudition	153
Daisy	43		
Damask	122	Fancy	191

INDEX OF WORDS.

	PAGE		PAGE
Favor	170	India	138
Florida	42	Indigo	122
Fortunate	70	Indolence	247
Frank	10, 107	Indolentia	158
Fuller	20	Ineptus	01
		Influence	130
Gamboge	122	Innocent	75
Gamin	100	Insult	244
Gaunt	20	Integrity	65
Gêne	85	Invidentia	150
German, Germany	138	Invidia	150
Giltcup	43	Irenæus	20
Gloze	78	Isothermal	150
Gnostic	120	Italy	130
Godsacre	51		
Golden knop	44	Jaberr	08
Golden rain	44	Jehovah	125
Gothic	115	Jet	122
Guillotine	165	Jove	125
Guinea	122	Jovial	130
Gypsy	124	Jutland	124
Habsburg	249	Karfunkel	47
Haft	236	Ketzer	170
Halcyon	46	Kickshaws	175
Hands	77	Kind	72
Happiness	70	Kingfisher	45
Heathen	104	Knave	68
Hermeneutics	134		
Hildebrand	27	Labarum	178
Honnêteté	85	Lady-bird	40
Huguenot	177	Legend	100
Humanitas	70	Lendemain	103
Humility	02	Leonine	181
Humour, humorous	128	Leopard	115
Hundred	259	Letters	232
Hurricane	120	Lewd	0
		Libertine	08
Idiot	85	Library	128
Idolatry	147	Lierre	103
Imbecile	245	Limbo	138
Impatientia	157	Limner	128
Impotens	60	Lingot	169
Incivisme	165	Lollard	170

INDEX OF WORDS.

	PAGE		PAGE
Long pig	80	Noyade	105
Love-child	80	Nun	108
Loyalty	204		
Lumber	127	Oblige, obligation	71
Lunacy	133	Obsequium	170
Luscinia	47	Occisissimus	167
Lutheran	110	Oculissimus	167
Macedonia	138	Pagan	103
Madeira	42	Pain	64
Magnet	122	Panic	133
Malevolentia	66	Panther	227
Mammet	112	Paper	128
Manes	28	Paradise	62
Manichæus	28	Paraffin	170
Mariposa	45	Parchment	122
Maudlin	68	Passion	60
Megrim	174	Pastime	7
Menial	68	Peace	80
Mercurial	130	Peach	123
Merkani	178	Peacock	227
Methodist	110, 204	Pelagius	28
Metrophanes	20	Perfide	85
Minion	68	Pfaffe	00
Miscreant	108	Pheasant	123
Miser	65	Philosopher	171
Mob	105	Phlegethon	42
Monachus	138	Phœbe	194
Monk	138	Piaculum	67
Mons Pileatus	48	Pict	125
Morbidezza	88	Pine apple	101
Morea	41	Plague	64
Morimo	10	Plantation	204
Mosaic	241	Plausible	50
Mulierositas	157	Poids	235
Muslin	123	Pois	235
		Poix	235
Naomi	25	Post	238
Natal	43	Potatoe	101
Naturalist	204	Prejudice, prejudicial	60, 61
Neutralization	153	Prime Minister	110
Norman	130	Prometheus	27
Novelist	204	Prude	73

INDEX OF WORDS.

	PAGE		PAGE
Prussian	130	Savage	234
		Sbirri	80
Quarantine	191	Schadenfreude	50
Querulous	87	Schlecht	74
Quick	240	Sclave	11
Quince	123	Scripture	255
		Sedakat	75
Rape	253	Self-sufficient	87
Rapture	6	Servator	148
Rationalist	172	Sham	105
Ravishment	8	Sherry	123
Razzia	105	Shire	236
Redeemer	258	Sierra	6
Reformation	117	Silly	75
Refugee	144	Simple	75
Regeneration	151	Sincere	245
Rejoice	80	Slave	11
Relaxation	247	Smith	230
Relent	244	Sodalicium	177
Religion	8	Soliloquium	170
Reprehend	245	Sorbonne	29
Resentment	50	Spaniel	123
Retaliation	60	Stellio	45
Retract	61	Stellionatus	40
Revelation	254	Stephen	20
Rhubarb	122	Sterling	123
Rivals	240	Sterry	28
Romantic	110	Stipulation	120
Rome	130	Stock	230
Rose-window	50	Styx	42
Rossignol	47	Subtle	245
Roué	104	Succinum	189
Roundhead	170	Sühnen	67
Rubric	131	Sünde	67
		Supercilious	245
Sacrament	105	Superstition	182
Sælig	75	Surname	250
Salutificator	140	Sycophant	182
Salvator	142	Synonym	185
Sanders	27		
Sarcasm	245	SYNONYMS.	
Sardonic	110	Abdicate, desert	213
Sarsnet	122	Abhor, detest, hate,	
Saturnine	110	loathe	201

INDEX OF WORDS.

	PAGE		PAGE
SYNONYMS.		Timeserver	58
Apprehend, comprehend	200	Tinsel	58
		Topaz	40
Arrogant, insolent, presumptuous	200	Tort	230
		Tory	119
Astrology, astronomy	197	Tragedy	121
Authentic, genuine	202, 203	Transliteration	154
Blanch, whiten	100	Transubstantiation	22, 198
Benefice, fief	217	Tribulation	30
Charity, love	100	Trinacria	40
Cloke, palliate	107	Trinity	138
Compulsion, obligation	211	Triticum	37
		Trivial	245
Congratulate, felicitate	206	Turkey	124
		Tyrant, tyranny	140
Contrary, opposite	210		
Despair, diffidence	108	Unitarian	117
Discover, invent	207	Urbanus	170
Education, instruction	212	Usignuolo	48
Enthusiasm, fanaticism	103	Vallenses	177
		Vane	28
Envy, emulation		Varlet	58
Fancy, imagination	101	Verb	243
Illegible, unreadable	100	Verres	28
Interference, interposition	190	Vigilantius	20
		Villain	58
Nave, ship	190	Virtue	72
Nay, no	100	Virtuoso	88
Revenge, vengeance	193	Virtus	88
Vindicta, ultio	193	Vocation	250
Yea, yes	100	Voluble	59
		Volume	128
Talent	70		
Tansy	174	Waldenses	177
Tawdry	50	Wales	250
Temper	129	Whig	119
Terrorism	105	Whit-sunday	178
Theocracy	147	Worsted	122
Thorpe	251	Worth, worthy	251
Thrall, thraldom	127	Wrong	230

Books by the same Author.

Notes on the Parables of Our Lord.
Tenth Edition, carefully revised. 8vo. cloth, 12s.

Notes on the Miracles of Our Lord.
Eighth Edition, carefully revised. 8vo. cloth, 12s.

Synonyms of the New Testament.
New Edition. One Vol. 8vo. cloth, 10s. 6d.

Proverbs and their Lessons.
Fifth Edition. fcp. 8vo. 3s.

Sermons preached in Westminster Abbey.
Second Edition. 8vo. 10s. 6d.

The Fitness of Holy Scripture for Unfolding the Spiritual Life of Man: Christ the Desire of all Nations;
Or, the Unconscious Prophecies of Heathendom. Hulsean Lectures. Fourth Edition. Fcp. 8vo. 5s.

On the Authorised Version of the New Testament.
Second Edition. 8vo. 7s.

Commentary on the Epistle to the Seven Churches in Asia.
Second Edition. 8vo. 8s. 6d.

Sacred Latin Poetry.
Chiefly Lyrical. Selected and arranged for Use. Second Edition, corrected and improved. Fcp. 8vo. 7s.

Books by the same Author.

Poems.
Collected and arranged anew. Fcp. 8vo. cloth, 7s. 6d.

Justin Martyr and other Poems.
Fifth Edition. Fcp. 8vo. 6s.

Poems from Eastern Sources, Genoveva, and other Poems.
Second Edition. Fcp. 8vo. 5s. 6d.

Elegiac Poems.
Third Edition. Fcp. 8vo. 2s. 6d.

Calderon's Life's a Dream:
The Great Theatre of the World. With an Essay on his Life and Genius. Fcp. 8vo. 4s. 6d.

Gustavus Adolphus' Social Aspect of the Thirty Years' War.
Fcp. 8vo. 2s. 6d.

English Past and Present.
Fifth Edition. Fcp. 8vo. 4s.

Select Glossary of English Words
Used formerly in Senses different from the Present. New Edition. Fcp. 8vo. cloth, 4s.

On some Deficiencies in our English Dictionaries.
Second Edition. 8vo. 3s.

MACMILLAN and CO. London.

www.ingramcontent.com/pod-product-compliance
Lightning Source LLC
Chambersburg PA
CBHW031251250426
43672CB00029BA/2096